KINGDOM
PROSPERITY

KINGDOM PROSPERITY

NOT WHAT YOU THINK

BARBARA GORE

LitPrime
"Your story is our priority"

LitPrime Solutions
21250 Hawthorne Blvd
Suite 500, Torrance, CA 90503
www.litprime.com
Phone: 1-800-981-9893

Published by LitPrime Solutions   03/01/2023

ISBN: 979-8-88703-153-8(sc)
ISBN: 979-8-88703-155-2(hc)
ISBN: 979-8-88703-154-5(e)

Library of Congress Control Number: 2023902080

Usually whenever people hear the word "prosperity", they think of money, houses, cars, boats, yachts, or other luxuries that the world hungers and longs for. Some may even think that God's "Kingdom Prosperity" is the same way. However, this book is written by the direction of the Holy Spirit to illuminate the truth of what God's "Kingdom Prosperity" really is! There is much more to it than worldly riches and what meets the eye!

CONTENTS

DEDICATION

I dedicate this book to my Lord and Savior, Jesus Christ, who has helped me to overcome a poverty mentality and shown me the true meaning of "Kingdom Prosperity".

Secondly, I dedicate this book to my readers, family, loved ones, and friends. I hope that your eyes of understanding will be opened to the truth of how to live truly prosperous and free! It is my heartfelt prayer, that because of this book, you will choose to enjoy true "Kingdom Prosperity" by living each and every day in God's will and His abundant blessings.

ACKNOWLEDGEMENTS

First of all, I want to thank my Lord Jesus Christ for my salvation, the precious Holy Spirit who lives within me, His unconditional love, undeserved mercy, and abundant grace. All of these blessings have helped me to get through the storms and trials in my life, which have given me the wisdom and knowledge that I share with you in this book.

I also want to thank my family, loved ones, and friends who have kept me in prayer all these years. Thank you for believing in me and the One who has given me this wonderful new life! A very special thank you to my pastors at Revival For Christ Club in Moore, OK, Church of the Harvest in Oklahoma City, OK, New Pilgrim Baptist Church in Salt Lake City, Utah, Cache Valley Christian Center in Logan, Utah, Victory Christian Center in Tulsa, OK, New Life Christian Center in Stigler, OK, Maranatha Christian Center in New Canton, IL, Pittsfield Assembly of God in Pittsfield, IL, and Oak Grove Harvest in Fred, TX. A very special thank you to Joyce Meyer of Joyce Meyer Ministries, who has been my spiritual mother since 1998! Thank you for teaching me the truth of the Word and how to walk and live victoriously in the will of God by following His plan for praying, fasting, and giving. Because of all of you, I now enjoy the abundant life Jesus died to give me and am living in true "Kingdom Prosperity"! May God bless you all richly!

INTRODUCTION

When the Lord spoke to me prophetically, through our youth pastor during an altar call, He said to write a book about prosperity, I was shocked and questioned in my heart whether the word truly came from the Lord. I was struggling to make ends meet even though my income was better than ever before. Like so many others, I lived from paycheck to paycheck, and had to rely on my faith in Jesus to help me get through each pay period.

"What do You mean by prosperity, Lord?" I asked as I was driving home after church.

Immediately He convicted me about my carnal way of thinking.

"Prosperity is much more than money, My child!" He answered. I apologized and repented quickly, asking for His forgiveness.

In the pages that follow, I will share with you the wonderful revelations of truth that the Lord has taught me through the Word of God and my personal experiences with Him about God's "Kingdom Prosperity".

I hope and pray this book will be a blessing to you, and that it will help you to understand how much different God's thoughts are from ours. May God bless you and enlighten you as you enjoy the journey!

CHAPTER 1
POVERTY MENTALITY

Due to circumstances beyond my control, throughout my childhood I became the victim of a poverty mentality. My biological father left our family when my mother was pregnant with me, so she was thrust into the very difficult role of being a single parent. I really don't remember much about the first three years of my life except that Mom worked outside our home to provide for my older sister and me, and I spent a lot of time at my grandmother's house.

Our lives were changed forever when Mom married our stepfather. Orin had never been married before and was nineteen years older than Mom. We were excited about our new family and our new "daddy". After I turned five, we moved to his farm back in the hills, about a mile off the main highway. Orin was very old-fashioned, and he didn't believe in modernization. We used coal oil lamps for light because we had no electricity, a single wood stove in the living room for heat, we hauled water from town to fill a cistern on our back porch, and Mom cooked on a stove in the kitchen, which used propane gas on one side, and the other side burned wood. Because we had no modern plumbing, we used an outhouse in the back yard, and we caught rain water from the eaves spouts in a long aluminum bathtub for our baths. We had no neighbors, so we took showers on the back porch whenever we were blessed with rain. This new life was rougher than we had imagined, but at least we were a whole family.

After the R.E.A. finally set poles and ran lines up our lane to bring electricity to us, I thought we were in heaven! Somehow, Mom and Orin scraped up enough money to get an old-fashioned wringer type washing machine, for which we heated water on the stove in a copper boiler. In the winter, I remember hanging our clothes on a line outside to dry, but they froze stiff before I got the clothespins on them. Our only transportation was an old pickup truck besides the work horses and a wagon. It was a real treat to get to go to my Aunt Wilma's house occasionally to make phone calls or to watch news on the television because we didn't have such luxuries at our home.

Our dairy herd began with two Brown Swiss cows, "Big Girl" and her daughter "Slow Poke". A little later, we added "Willow", another Brown Swiss cow. We milked them all by hand, chilled the milk, skimmed off the cream, and sold it to make a few dollars. Orin sold hogs to get the essentials, but there wasn't much left for anything else. Farming was hard work as we started our day at four a.m. milking the cows, feeding the hogs, and doing other chores. After we cleaned up and ate breakfast, we walked down the mile long lane to meet the school bus, no matter what the weather was. As soon as we got home from school, we did our chore routine all over again before supper, and then we studied for the next day's school assignments.

When school wasn't in session, I went with my stepfather to the fields with a team of horses and horse drawn equipment. I helped him shuck corn, bale hay, or whatever else there was to do. One particular day, I remember going to the corn field with him to shuck corn when there was so much mud, we could hardly walk. He and I had shucked a wagon full of corn. When we got to the end of the row, the horses balked and wouldn't move either way because the wagon was so heavy.

It had sunk down in the mud so deep that they had trouble pulling it. Orin had an explosive temper, so when the horses didn't move, he started beating them with a whip. Suddenly, one of them went one way and the other horse went the opposite way overturning the whole wagon load of corn in the mud. Orin was so angry that he jumped up and down cursing and stomping the helmet that he wore all the time. He was a very large man, weighing over three-hundred pounds, and standing over six feet tall. This scenario appeared to be so funny to me that I took off across the corn field to hide and laugh. I knew better than to laugh in front of him, but I just couldn't hold it back.

Our huge gardens always required a lot of work and time from start to finish; but we were thankful to have food on our table, especially in the wintertime. We canned a lot of fruit and vegetables, butchered our own hogs, dressed our chickens for meat to put on the table, and sold eggs from our chickens and guineas.

I will never forget the special times we enjoyed together during the Christmas season. Mom and we girls spent hours baking cookies, pies, and making candy to give away as gifts for our family, neighbors, and friends. Each year we went to the pasture or the woods to pick out a Christmas tree, chop it down, and drag it back to the house so we could decorate it. Making our own decorations for the tree from tin foil, coloring crayons and paper, and stringing popcorn for garlands provided many enjoyable hours of quality family time. Mom and Orin sold hogs or whatever they had so that they could get us each a pair of coveralls or shoes for our Christmas gifts. We were always delighted to get them.

Homemade gifts were a real blessing, especially the Topsy-Eva doll Mom made for me. She had a pink face and yellow yarn for hair on one end (Eva), and a brown face with black yarn for hair when you flipped her over (Topsy). She was very special to me since toys were always a treat, and Mom had sewn every stitch with love for me. We prepared our Christmas dinner together, blessed it, and then sat down as a family to enjoy some fellowship and a bountiful feast. Those hours we spent together as a family are some of the most precious memories I have. Now, I realize how rich I was, even though everything about our lifestyle shouted "poverty".

As I grew up, my self-esteem plummeted as my heart and dreams shattered into a million pieces. I couldn't understand why my stepfather abused me verbally, emotionally, and physically all the time when I hadn't done anything to deserve it. I never told Mom about the abuse because I feared making it worse. The insults hurled at me by my peers and classmates at school added to my lack of confidence. Because I didn't have nice clothing and couldn't afford the things they had, they degraded me by calling me "that poor little farm girl". I began to believe that I was just what they said I was. I saw myself as hopeless, helpless, lacking, and in poverty. Self-pity and frustration enveloped my life with a cloud of darkness that blocked any rays of hope from me. I often wondered what it would be like if my natural dad had been in the picture, but I strongly doubted that I would ever get to meet him.

Everything I had heard about him was so negative that I wasn't sure I wanted to see him at all. So, I just retreated inside myself, holding in all those years of anger, bitterness, and resentment for all that I felt I had been cheated out of.

Mom taught us to always bless our food before we ate, what was right and wrong, and how to pray at bedtime, but her personal belief in God seemed to be a secret she never shared with us. She told me a few Bible stories, but that was mostly the extent of what I knew about God, except when I went to church with Grandma and Grandpa. I imagined God to be some giant being, waiting for me to do something wrong so He could bring down a big hammer of judgment upon me and condemn me to hell. I'm not quite sure where that came from, but I did have a fear of the Lord that was too great for this little girl to understand. I knew that I didn't want Him to be angry with me. Grandpa taught me that giving an offering in church was important, and each Sunday when I went to church with him and Grandma, he gave me some pennies to put in the offering plate as it was passed. My first known conviction from the Lord came when I was five years old. Donna, Grandpa's daughter from a previous marriage, went to church with us that Sunday morning. Before we left the house, Donna and I had talked about how badly we wanted some peanuts to share after church. Since we didn't know if Grandpa would give us the money to buy them or not, we devised a plan. I would put my pennies in the offering plate, but she would keep hers to buy peanuts. I felt bad about even thinking that way, but at that tender age, my burning desire for the peanuts overrode my sense of wrong. So I went along with the plan. After church, we ran ahead of Grandma and Grandpa, and went to the little service station across the street from their home. We bought our peanuts and were really enjoying them when Grandpa suddenly showed up. He stood there looking at us with that certain look that told us that we were really in trouble.

"Where did you girls get the money for those peanuts?" he asked.

We both stood still, frozen with fright until finally, Donna spoke up. "I spent my pennies for them, Daddy. Sandy, (my nickname at that time), put hers in the offering plate and I kept mine to buy the peanuts".

You could have heard a pin drop. Then Grandpa, in his stern but loving voice said, "Do you girls realize you have just stolen from the Lord?"

Suddenly, I completely lost my appetite for the peanuts. I shook violently as I waited for the strong arm of the Lord to come down on me like a hammer. I hadn't thought of our little scheme as "stealing from the Lord", but it really was because the pennies were meant to be given to Him.

"You need to apologize to the Lord and ask Him to forgive you now! I would have given you money for peanuts if you would have asked me", was his response.

We both quickly told the Lord we were sorry and promised that we wouldn't ever do that again. I felt the burden lift and breathed a big sigh of relief. This was the beginning of wisdom for me, and I can honestly say, I never even thought about trying that again.

Grandpa and Grandma often took Donna and me with them on their summer vacations. I was so blessed to enjoy staying at motels, eating in restaurants, swimming in real pools, and sending cards back home to my family to let them know I was having a good time. Unfortunately, after the vacation was over, it was back to reality again.

When I was eight, Mom started having a second family with my stepfather. The firstborn was a son, our brother John, who had dark hair and the most beautiful sparkling brown eyes I had ever seen. They seemed to dance with joy. My sister Betty and I were delighted to have a baby brother and we really loved him. After two years, our sister Carol was born, and less than two years later, our brother Orin arrived on the scene. Our brother Frank came along a little later on. This new family increased my responsibilities because I had to help take care of them, while Mom drove my stepfather around to do whatever they needed to do, such as taking care of business, shopping, or going to Orin's father's farm to work. I loved my brothers and sisters deeply, but I missed Mom being there to help out. Soon, the overwhelming pressure of being a big sister hit me hard.

After my older sister Betty turned sixteen, she was stricken with polio. She was in a hospital in St. Louis for an extended period of time, lingering on the edge of life and death. With the help of God, many prayers, and a lot of encouragement from the staff at the hospital, she survived. Mom spent many hours helping her with physical therapy after she came home. Because of Betty's handicap, the school bus finally began coming up our lane. Betty eventually moved into our Aunt Naomi's home so that she could have access to the modern conveniences she needed. She excelled in school, becoming a "straight A student". I made good grades but wasn't as excellent a student as her former teachers expected me to be, so my lack of self-confidence increased.

"You will never amount to anything!" my stepfather frequently commented. "You can't do anything right!" he often added to the former remarks.

After Betty graduated from high school, she went to college at the University of Illinois where she later met her husband, Ken. When they got married, I was honored to be her bridesmaid. I remember momentarily feeling a little spark of envy, as I thought to myself, *"How great it must be to have someone to care enough about you to want to spend the rest of his life with you!"*

As my high school graduation drew near, I began thinking more seriously about what I wanted to do with my life. I had always wanted to be a nurse, so I started checking into scholarships that I could get to pay for my training. When I applied for admission to the Passavant Hospital School of Nursing in Jacksonville, Illinois, I was accepted. I received a grant from the State of Illinois for my training with the stipulation that I work for the state for three years after graduation. Finally, I could see some glimmer of light at the end of the tunnel, as something positive started happening on the horizon of my future.

CHAPTER 2
BREAKING AWAY

After graduation from high school, I began preparations to leave the farm to go to nurses training in the fall. I didn't know how long it would be before I could go visit anyone after I started my training. After talking it over with Mom, I decided to visit some of my family while I could. One of those family members was my Aunt Pauline, my biological father's sister. Since Betty had polio, Aunt Pauline and several of Dad's family members tried to make up for Dad leaving us the way he did. When I asked Mom about visiting Aunt Pauline, she told me that I would have to call her first to be sure it was all right. We still didn't have a telephone so my stepfather and I went to town to Grandma's house to call her.

"Aunt Pauline, this is Sandy. I am going to nurse's training this fall and was wondering if I could come visit you tonight for a couple of days," I asked.

"I don't know" she said, "your dad is due in from Montana tomorrow and I don't know how your mom feels about you being here while he is here. If she doesn't care I don't mind, but you will have to ask her and do whatever she says".

I was numb with shock for a little while, trying to comprehend what she had just said to me. I had no idea that my father ever came back to

Illinois to visit. I thanked Grandma for letting me use her phone and slowly walked to the truck where Orin waited for me.

"What did she say?" he asked. I reluctantly told him about my dad coming to Aunt Pauline's house because I felt quite sure I knew what his response would be. He sat quietly for a few moments, and then calmly asked me, "So how do you feel about meeting your real dad?"

I didn't want to make him angry but I knew he genuinely wanted to know. "I would like to meet him and form my own opinion if that is all right with Mom and you."

After that, there was silence until we got back to the farm. As soon as I walked in the house, Mom asked me, "Well, what are you going to do?"

I really didn't want to let her know about my dad being there, but she had always taught me to tell the truth, no matter what the consequences were. "My dad is coming to Aunt Pauline's tomorrow," I said timidly.

As I expected, she immediately responded hatefully, "You aren't going there to be with him!" Those old feelings of abandonment and rejection that surfaced within her rekindled her anger against him. I was devastated by her response, but I knew enough to keep my mouth shut and respect her decision.

"Now just wait a minute, Edna! I think at seventeen years old, if she wants to meet her dad and get to know him for herself, she should have that right!" my stepfather retaliated. He had never gone against anything Mom said regarding us girls before, and it shocked me that he stood up for my desires. I just stood there stunned for a moment, waiting for her to say something else, but instead Orin looked at me and nodded. "Go pack your things and I will take you to your Aunt Pauline's!"

I hesitated, waiting for more confrontation, but to my surprise, there wasn't any. So I packed a bag for a couple of days, and we headed out the door. When we got in the pickup, I thanked Orin for giving me the opportunity to meet my dad. The rest of the trip was very quiet, and the only thing he said was, "Have a good time," as I got out of the truck to go into Aunt Pauline's house.

The next morning, we were all sitting at the breakfast table when Dad and his family drove up the lane to Aunt Pauline's house. Part of me wanted to run and hide while another part of me wanted to run into his arms. I was frozen in my seat, not knowing what to do. When he came into the kitchen, Aunt Pauline pointed me out and said, "Fay, do you know who this is?"

He stood there looking at me with a stunned gaze and responded, "Is this Sandy?" She confirmed it to him and without hesitation he threw his arms open wide to receive my hug. Then she introduced me to his wife Evelyn, his daughter Linda, and his son Paul. Wow! I surely hadn't expected anything like this!

Dad and I spent most of the day walking, talking, and getting acquainted after all the years that had been stolen from us. This was the first time we had ever laid eyes on each other and it was a little awkward at first. I was happy when he opened up to share his side of the story with me. I was surprised that he felt comfortable enough to tell me. He told me that he was as much to blame for the breakup as anyone, but that he and Mom were both very young when they got married. Dad had fought in World War II, so he had many war scars that needed a lot of emotional healing. I sensed the true love of my father that day, and realized that even though I didn't know him, I loved him. It was a special bond that only God could create. After I went to nursing school, Dad and I wrote to each other regularly. We had a wonderful relationship and I looked forward to visiting him in Montana sometime.

I enjoyed nursing school, especially when I started being a "hands on" nursing student and was caring for real people in real life situations. I had finally found something I could do right and it felt so great to help others.

I had been there only three months when I met Paul and soon, we started dating. We fell in love so quickly that at Christmas, he asked me to marry him, and gave me an engagement ring. We planned to be married in August 1965 after my capping ceremony. I intended to finish nursing school even though I was married. Paul took me home to visit Mom and meet my family at Christmas in 1964. Together we made our announcement that we were engaged to be married the next year. My stepfather just looked at me, and then back to Paul. He said, "You'd better take good care of her!"

Mom was very unhappy about my choice. She looked at me and firmly said, "You are not getting married until you finish nursing school!" This sharp authoritative statement quickly aroused rebellion in this eighteen-year-old "know it all" girl. Because I respected Mom and had been taught to control my anger in her sight, I held back until we headed back to Jacksonville. Inwardly, I was boiling.

A little tormenting voice just kept haunting me with, "*You are eighteen and you can do whatever you want to! She can't stop you!*" I continually listened to this evil voice because I didn't know how to shut it up and I couldn't shake it off.

One night in early June, on a date with Paul, I told Him, "Let's just go ahead and get married now!" "*I only have three days until my doctor's appointment to get my birth control pills, so I know that everything will be all right,*" I thought to myself. We were both tired of waiting and we wanted this marriage more than anything else, so he quickly agreed. During the next few days, we bought the marriage license and took our blood tests. A few days later, we were married in a private ceremony in the home of a Justice of the Peace in Jacksonville, Illinois. We immediately moved in with Paul's parents until we could find a place of our own that we could afford.

CHAPTER 3
A NEW STRUGGLE

Our season of staying with Paul's parents proved to be quite a challenge, but we were thankful for a place to share our new life together. His father had dementia so he lived in his own little world most of the time. His mother didn't care much for me because I had "stolen her baby boy." She was always drinking when she said those things, but her words cut through my heart like a knife. I wanted so much to be accepted and welcomed into her life!

We finally found a little two-room home of our own, but now we had another problem. I was already pregnant before I got the chance to start my birth control pills, so I had to pay the consequences. I struggled through the following weeks of morning sickness, which ended up lasting all day long, while trying to get through my nurse's training. One morning, while caring for one of my patients, I suddenly became extremely nauseated and had to exit his room quickly. As I ran down the hallway to the bathroom, I met my instructor. "Please send someone to take care of my patient!" I cried out as we passed one another. After she found someone to care for him, she came to find me.

"Barbara is there something that you need to tell me?" she inquired.

"Yes, ma'am, I'm pregnant," I openly but reluctantly admitted. "I really want to finish my training anyway, if I may," I said timidly with tears in my eyes. My self-esteem plummeted even farther because I realized that I had made the wrong choice by not waiting to get married. The school let me complete my first year, but the doctor made it plain that I couldn't do anything strenuous during my pregnancy.

After our oldest son Nick was born and was six weeks old, I was released to go back to work. I started working as a nurse aide at the hospital where I had taken my nurse's training. I found that I could apply the knowledge I had gained from nursing school, and I enjoyed helping others. I worked a year and three months until we conceived my second son Danny. Once again, the doctors advised me not to work during my pregnancy, so I quit my job to stay home with Nick. This pregnancy was more difficult for me than the first one because Paul couldn't keep a job to support us. We fought continuously over money and other petty little issues. We had to depend on others to help us out with food and finances, which was very frustrating to me.

Right after Danny was born, Paul came to the hospital to visit. He had a great big smile on his face, and handed me a set of car keys. "What are these to?" I inquired.

"It's your Easter present," he replied. He told me that he had landed another good job, and had bought me the car of my dreams. It was a 1965 Chevrolet Impala, metal flake orchid in color with a black interior and a four speed shift in the floor. At first, I was angry because I knew that meant another payment to try to make each month. After I thought about it a little while, I knew that this was his way of showing me that he loved and appreciated me. I believe it was also a kind of peace offering to make up for all the recent arguments we had.

As soon as the doctor released me to return to work, I started to work as a nurse aide at the hospital in Jacksonville. My new job was a twenty mile journey one way. One morning in the darkness right before dawn, as I topped a hill, my headlights caught something wet on the highway at the foot of the hill. Automatically, I hit the brake and suddenly, the car started spinning wildly out of control in the middle of a huge oil spill from an overturned tanker. At one point, I looked up and saw a telephone pole directly in front of me and the car was headed right for it. With my foot frozen on the brake in fear, all I could do was to scream out "Oh, Jesus!" Immediately, the car stopped on the opposite side of the road on the shoulder facing oncoming traffic, but it hadn't hit anything. I was badly shaken, but I knew in my heart that the hand of God had been with me in this frightening episode. I was very thankful. This should have opened my eyes, but I continued to live my life my own way, without realizing how truly blessed I was to have the Lord on my side.

After this incident Paul lost his job. So our arguments heightened to such intensity that I started having real emotional problems. Our marriage was on very shaky ground. We had stopped putting the Lord first in our lives and my life was crumbling around me. Someone had told me that Paul was cheating on me, so I thought to myself *"Two can play that game!"*

One evening, when Paul was working late, a friend asked me to take her to Hillview to see her boyfriend, so I agreed. As she got out of the car to go into his house, I jokingly said, "If he has a cute brother, send him out." She took me seriously and sent his older brother Don out to meet me. I took one look into his beautiful sparkling baby blue eyes and was swept away by his sweet mannerism. As we talked a little while that night, I found the comfort and compassion that I was missing at home.

When our sons were one and three years old and they had gone to bed one night, Paul and I had a terrible argument. It escalated into such a heavy fight that I lost control of my emotions, many of which had been stored up from my childhood abuse. I angrily grabbed a cast iron skillet and had it positioned right above Paul's head, with every intention of hitting him with all my strength.

This horrible demonic plan was interrupted suddenly when my oldest son Nick screamed at the top of his lungs, "Mommy, don't hurt my daddy!"

Shocked and stunned, I snapped to my senses and all I could think was *"Get out of here before you kill him!"* I threw the skillet across the room, grabbed my car keys, ran from the house, and spun out of the driveway like a maniac.

During the next few terrifying miles, as I thought about and realized what I had almost done, I lost all connections with reality. All I knew was that I had to get away from Paul, and the only place of refuge I could think of was Don's parents' house. On the way to Hillview, as I rapidly approached a very sharp curve, with a steep ravine on both sides, I glanced down at the speedometer and noticed it was buried past 120 miles per hour. Instinctively, I slammed on the brakes, and by the grace of God, the car never rolled over as it normally would have. As I look back now, there is no doubt that this was another wake-up call from the Lord, but I didn't heed it either. As I pulled up in front of Don's parents' house, I slammed on the brakes and skidded to a halt on the gravel. He came running out to see what was going on. Trembling all over, I explained to him what had happened and told him I didn't know what to do. I was horrified!

I deeply loved Paul and my sons, but I just couldn't deal with our broken marriage any longer. I slept on the couch alone that night. The next day when I awakened, I was overwhelmed with guilt and shame. I could hardly stand myself, much less go back to face Paul and the boys. I was extremely confused and so appalled by my behavior and my intentions that I knew something terrible had happened to me. At that moment in time, I believed that God was so angry with me that

He would never hear another prayer. I certainly didn't feel that I was worthy of talking to Him, let alone asking for forgiveness. So I chose to try to work through this situation on my own.

I pondered what would happen to the boys if I were to go get them to be with me. Suddenly, I realized I had no place to take them, and no one to care for them while I worked. *"They do have a home with Paul, and the house payments are low enough he can make them somehow. At least they have a shelter over their heads and food to eat,"* I thought. My mind was like a giant racetrack with horrible thoughts and fears colliding, running rampant without any solid direction and fear was overwhelming me. Reality was setting in and depression hovered over me like a huge storm cloud.

I stayed at Don's parents' home for a couple of days before I decided to go back home to see the boys and to get some clean clothes to wear. I prepared myself for a major confrontation with Paul as I drove back to Roodhouse. Surprisingly, when I got there, everyone was gone and the doors and windows were nailed shut. I drove over to my mother-in-law's home, but my friend from across the street met me outside before I went to the door. "Where are my boys?" I asked frantically.

"I can't tell you, Barb," she responded. She was sworn to secrecy. I angrily spun out of the driveway and drove back to the house that once had been our home. I struggled anxiously but my key no longer worked in the lock, so in a rage of anger, frustration, and desperation I broke the door open, ran inside, and quickly grabbed some clean clothes. I climbed back into my car, slammed the door, and sped away toward Hillview where I had been staying.

As I was driving through White Hall, a policeman pulled me over and asked to see my driver's license. When he looked at it and saw who I was, he said, "Ma'am, get out of the car and come go with me!"

"Why?" I anxiously asked him, my heart pounding and my whole body shaking.

"You have been reported as a missing person! I can't let you go until you call your Aunt Wilma so she can let your mother know where you are." Reluctantly, I locked my car, climbed into the squad car and went to the police station with him.

Paul had called Aunt Wilma, upsetting her and the whole family. When I called her she proceeded to give me the third degree. I told her I was fine and asked her to let Mom know I would be contacting her soon.

While I was sitting in the police station, the report came in over the police radio that Paul's home had been broken into. I quickly admitted to the officer that it was me who had broken in because the doors and windows had been nailed shut, and I needed clean clothing to wear. I was almost ready to leave the police station to go back to my car when another officer brought Paul in to talk to me. He begged me to come back as he promised that everything would be different if I would just come back home. I told him that I needed time to think things through and I would call him in a couple of days.

I stayed in Hillview a couple of days longer as I tried to figure out what to do. Guilt and condemnation overwhelmed me for leaving my sons and my husband but I was too stubborn to ask God to forgive me and help me. *"God will never forgive me for being so stupid!"* I thought as I pondered the situation. Then I became angry with God for allowing me to do such a thing as stinking thinking filled my troubled mind. Finally, I made a decision to go back and try to make our marriage work so that I could be a mother to our sons.

Paul was very happy to have me back home again, but trusting one another was a big issue. The tension in our relationship was so great that it seemed like a heavy storm cloud surrounding us as the whole atmosphere changed for the worse. I knew in my heart that our marriage was over and I couldn't live there anymore. I found an apartment nearby in White Hall and made arrangements with Paul to visit with the boys at my apartment every other weekend when I was off work. I picked them up on Friday evenings and took them back home on Sunday afternoons.

Without inviting God to help me, I was struggling all alone to make ends meet and living in a world of self-pity, anger, and defeat. Guilt and shame continued to rule my life to keep me away from the only One who could really help me and set me free. I couldn't bring myself to go to church or to even pray because I felt so ashamed and condemned over my choices.

CHAPTER 4
MOVING ON WITH MY LIFE

D on and I started dating but it wasn't long before our fleshly desires consumed us, so we got a place of our own and started living together. He and his father ran a salvage yard and I continued to work as a nurse aide. I still went to Paul's house to get the boys every other weekend for visitation.

When they came down, we visited Don's family or enjoyed doing something special as a family. Don and I were deeply in love but we decided not to get married until we knew it would work out. He had been married and divorced twice before but had never had any children of his own. I continued to have a deep sense of guilt and felt "too dirty" to even approach God with prayer.

After our divorce, Paul met, dated, and married another woman. She and I got along great, and I was happy knowing that the boys once more had a "complete family". That tended to ease my own guilt somewhat, but in my heart and mind I was continually tormented by the evil that I had allowed to dictate my life.

After Don and I had lived together for a couple of years, I became acutely aware of a longing for a child of his own. Without praying about it, discussing it, or Don's knowledge, I stopped my birth control and became pregnant. I didn't realize that Don and his family thought he couldn't have any children. Neither of his other wives had become pregnant, so this really caused some problems between us. He didn't know that they had both taken birth control pills without his knowledge. I thought surely he would be happy about this pregnancy and marry me immediately. I didn't know that his divorce from his second wife wasn't final yet. When I told him that I was pregnant, he started drinking very heavily and avoiding being with me. He and his family thought I had cheated on him and the baby couldn't possibly be his. As they constantly discussed our situation among themselves, it only made matters worse. Doubt and mistrust overwhelmed him as my pregnancy continued.

My doctors told me not to work while I was pregnant so the responsibility for paying the bills rested on Don's shoulders. He began spending most of his time in the bars drinking up the money he had and flirting with other women. Immense emotional pain and strife overshadowed our relationship as our situation became worse day by day. Even though I prepared special meals for him and kept our home spotless, he still didn't want to spend any time with me. Finally, one night, when I was almost seven months pregnant, I had all I could take. So in a fit of anger and rage, I went to the bar to find him. When he didn't acknowledge me when I spoke to him, I made the horrible mistake of slapping him in the face and cursing him. I immediately found myself in the floor across the room, as he came charging at me like a bull. The bartender immediately grabbed him and told me to get out of there, so I left. Once again I found myself losing touch with reality, with extreme anger, frustration, and desperation overwhelming my soul.

When I left the bar, I returned home to find his younger brother Jack waiting there to console me. When Don wasn't home by around two in the morning, I couldn't sleep. I decided to go find him. Jack and I got into my car and cruised around the town. We found him in front of a house flirting with two other women. I slammed on the brakes, intending to jump out to confront them all, but Jack quickly hit the gas pedal to get me out of there.

After we got home, Jack said to me, "Don isn't worth all this trouble and you really need to calm down and let him go!" After Jack left I went to bed but lay awake waiting for Don to get home as I plotted what I could do to him to get even.

When he finally came home around 4 a.m., I pretended to be asleep until he got into bed. The minute he crawled into bed, I told him in no uncertain terms, "I have had quite enough of this life and you have a choice to make! It is either me and your child or your booze and your other women!"

I let him sleep on that thought. A couple of days later, he sincerely apologized to me. "I'm very sorry, Barb, for all the pain I have caused you! If I had my divorce from Pat, I would marry you in a minute! I want and need you and my baby more than anything else!" He didn't have the money for the divorce, so after some discussion, I borrowed the money from his Uncle Walter to proceed with it. Don obtained an attorney and soon his divorce from Pat was finalized.

Shortly after that I started having some complications with my pregnancy and was hospitalized. One morning the doctor told me that I had to make a critical decision about my life and the life of our baby. The odds were against success no matter which way I decided, so I called Don to talk to him. He wasn't available at that moment. Seeking some much needed comfort and reassurance, I called Mom.

I explained the critical choices I had to make but I didn't expect her to show up that day because she lived about sixty miles from the hospital. Around noon she came into my room very angry with me for registering under Don's last name because we weren't married yet. I hadn't expected her to be upset with me because I thought surely she understood that I needed reassurance and comfort. Instead she put me down for living with Don without being married to him and for not taking care of the children I already had. I instantly responded with painful indignation and said some very hurtful things to her, which I soon regretted. I had been taught to have respect for my parents no matter what they said or did.

Right after that the nurse came in and told Mom, "Ma'am, You will have to step out because her husband is here." Mom went to the waiting room without hesitancy and Don came into the room. It wasn't long before he had to leave the room too because the fetal monitor showed that the baby was in distress due to all the stress I was under.

I thought to myself, *"Now, look at the mess you have made out of all these lives!"* As condemnation hit me like a ton of bricks I blamed myself for everything and I became very depressed. After the fetal distress subsided and I had calmed down, the nurse let Don return to the room.

"What happened out there in the waiting room?" I asked.

"I think your mom and I understand each other now," he answered. In a few moments, he left to go back to the salvage yard and Mom came back to the room with a whole new attitude. She apologized to me as I did to her and we both asked each other's forgiveness. She gave me a hug and left to go back home saying she would be seeing me.

Don returned that evening to discuss the life and death decision we needed to make regarding the baby within my womb. "We have to make a choice to let me carry the baby longer or to have them take the baby by Cesarean Section now," I explained. "My body is building antibodies against the baby which could kill it. Our blood types have incompatible Rh factors which are causing all the problems," I further explained to him. We carefully weighed the pros and cons and together we decided I would try to carry the baby a little longer to give the baby more of a chance of developing more completely. The next morning I shared our decision with my doctor, knowing that either way this little life within me was very precious and special.

When I was discharged from the hospital we got our marriage license and had a private little ceremony at a minister's home. Twelve days later, at eight months of pregnancy, the doctors determined that my antibody count was too high to let me carry the baby any longer. They scheduled a Cesarean Section to try to save both our lives.

For the next three days after my surgery, I was in and out of reality, heavily sedated so that I wouldn't worry. Sandy, our new baby daughter underwent two complete blood exchange transfusions in the first forty-eight hours of her life, as she battled to stay alive. I vaguely remember Don standing at my bedside, squeezing my hand with tears filling his eyes. On the fourth day the doctors decreased my sedation, and I was allowed to walk with help to the nursery window to view our precious tiny daughter as she lay under a special bilirubin light. She was so beautiful, I longed to hold her but she couldn't be out from under that special light yet. At least she was alive and fighting to stay that way.

When I finally got to hold her for a short time on the fifth day, the first thing I did was to count her fingers and toes. She was perfect in every way and she looked just like Don, which was an answer to my daily prayer to the Lord. I realized He had blessed us with a miracle but I still wasn't ready to surrender totally to Him. In my desperation, I had cried out to Him to help and He had graciously answered my prayers. I now understand how His heart must have broken as I continued my rebellious journey to live life my own way, especially after the miracle He had just given us.

Sandy quickly became the apple of her daddy's eye, as well as the rest of the family's. She stole their hearts and as she grew, she could do no wrong in their eyes. I went back to work on the night shift so

Don let her sleep in our bed because he was afraid he wouldn't hear her during the night if she awakened.

When she was five months old, I started L.P.N. school with credits for the courses I had taken in my first year of R.N. school. So I was able to graduate quickly. Upon graduation, I took on my first job as an L.P.N. on the night shift at the local hospital. The night shift was the only position available to me, so as Don continued to let Sandy sleep with him, our marriage relationship deteriorated rapidly. That little tormenting voice kept whispering in my ear, *"She is taking your place in your bed, in your marriage, and in your life!"* Soon, I started to resent my own daughter. Satan had a real stronghold on my mind and I had no idea of how to break it. I was too stubborn to pray and ask the Lord to take over my life because I wanted to live my way. I chose to continue to pay the price. Sandy was around two years old when we finally agreed to make her start sleeping in her own bed. I wasn't allowed to correct her without getting in trouble with Don or his family. I felt that I was on a sinking ship with no life raft. Both of her older brothers loved her dearly but she caused them trouble with her daddy nearly all the time. They too started to resent her and the favoritism Don showed her.

I became restless and very unhappy with my job at the hospital. When a position opened up in Jacksonville at a new nursing home, I jumped on the opportunity. I struggled daily with depression and often contemplated suicide because I was so tormented. In fact, sometimes I actually attempted to crash the car into a telephone pole or a tree on the way to work, hoping to end it all but it never worked. My overwhelming depression and emotional distress hadn't ever affected my job performance as a nurse, I didn't think. One evening when I was on duty and an older gentleman refused to take his medication, I lost control and yelled at him. Just as soon as that happened, the director of nursing, who was working late that evening, came into the room, and placed her hand on my shoulder.

"Barbara, come go to my office with me now, please!" I felt sure that she was going to fire me over this incident. After she found another nurse to take care of my patients, she quietly and sweetly said to me, "Have a seat here in my office and let's talk. Tell me, what is so terrible in your life?"

Even though I tried to hold back, it all came out like a flood. "I hate my daughter, I hate my husband, and I hate my life," I answered with tears streaming down my cheeks. I went on to tell her about the tormenting voices I heard all the time and my desire to end it all because I felt that no one loved me anymore.

After sitting quietly and compassionately listening for what seemed like hours, she said to me, "I want you to get some counseling for your depression, Barbara. You are too good of a nurse to lose and to let you go through this all by yourself. I know that the person I heard yelling tonight just wasn't the Barbara I know and love! It was totally out of your character to lose control with a patient, so I know that you need help desperately!" When I agreed to this, she scheduled an appointment for me with the local counseling center. She even offered to take me if I wanted her to. I agreed to attend biweekly sessions with a mental health counselor and to start taking antidepressants. Each day when I got to work, Ginny met me in the hall and took me to her office for our daily chat. I was amazed that she cared so much about me and that she kept me on the job after that little incident.

Soon after I started counseling, Don started drinking again. "I just can't deal with a wife who has mental problems," he said. This only added to my depression, lack of confidence, and frustration.

After his father died in 1978, he closed the salvage yard because people who bought cars and parts on credit from him wouldn't pay.

He no longer had any desire to do anything but drink and hang out in the bars. Our fights escalated as I felt more of a burden to make a living for all three of us and our relationship continued to deteriorate rapidly. We wouldn't argue in front of our daughter because I was determined that she would not hear us fight continuously, (like my sons had experienced with my first marriage). I began looking for a better paying job and soon landed a position with the state of Illinois at the Alton Mental Health Center.

After I started working there, we moved to East Alton for a short time and then on to Brighton, where we bought a house contract for deed. The pay and benefits were great but the stress level was horrendous, both on the job and at home. I worked on a closed unit with mentally retarded adults and the physical attacks against the workers were phenomenal. There were a lot of call-offs from staff members to avoid the abuse from the patients which created a hardship on those of us who were already there. I often ended up working sixteen-hour shifts because the other employees wouldn't answer their phones to come in to work when someone else called in.

When Sandy was eight years old she was quite out of control because I wasn't allowed to discipline her. Feelings of helplessness, hopelessness, and depression were my constant companions as they encompassed me like a great fog. I felt as if my life was spinning out of control. My dad died in the early fall of 1980 and we had to have our long-time precious poodle, Mitzi, put to sleep shortly after that. My world was slowly crumbling around me and I felt that I was losing ground but I kept on pushing myself until I was so tired I could barely stand it.

The day after Thanksgiving in 1980, while on duty, one of the patients broke my right little finger. I couldn't get anyone to cover my shift so I had to bear it out until my shift ended to go to the emergency room. The doctor placed me off work on workman's compensation for six weeks to allow it time to heal. This didn't help our finances because I received only part of what I normally made, but at least, I had something coming in.

After I went back to work, I found that my stress level increased remarkably because I was afraid of being hurt again. Things at home weren't improving either. However, I kept that job because I really couldn't afford to take less money working any place else.

CHAPTER 5
MY CRASHING WORLD

Over the next few months my stress level continued to build steadily and my depression increased tremendously. Finally, while I was on duty at work, on April 15, 1981 my world came crashing down around me. Suddenly I lost all sense of reality, collapsed onto the floor, and broke out into uncontrollable sobs with tears streaming down my face not knowing who I was, where I was, or why I was even there. I had absolutely no comprehension of what was happening to me and I really didn't care. The next few hours are lost somewhere in space and time. I don't even remember how I got back to my home in Brighton. When I returned to a slight state of awareness, my husband was calling my psychiatrist in Alton. After Don hung up the telephone, he loaded me into the car and took me to a hospital in Florissant, Missouri where I was immediately admitted to a locked psychiatric unit.

My psychiatrist told me that I had experienced a complete mental breakdown and had been diagnosed with bipolar disorder. I spent the next month in the hospital in intense psychotherapy, private and group counseling, treatment with psychotropic medications, and assertiveness training. It was a long, tedious, and painful journey back to reality but I had the best of care, therapists, and psychiatrists. My prognosis was guarded, and I wasn't sure that I would ever recover enough to face the world or life again. The hospital became my safe haven, away from the pain of the outside world. Whenever I was allowed to leave for outings for a full day, fear gripped my mind and my heart until I got back inside those locked doors. Everything seemed so different now; my family members were like strangers to me.

"When is the doctor going to let you come home? Why is he keeping you here so long?" Don angrily fired away at me when he came to visit me after I had been a patient there for about a month.

With the new assertiveness training that I had been given I was able to muster up the courage to keep my calm attitude. I replied, "If you want to know all these things, why don't you call him yourself in the morning when he is in the office? I'm sure he would be glad to answer them for you."

This new approach and response to his anger invoked some strange looks from him as he asked himself the question, "What have they done to her?" Needless to say, our visit didn't last very long that evening because he just didn't know how to handle the new person I was becoming.

The next morning, when my doctor came to visit me, he told me that Don had called him that morning and he had set the record straight for him. "Whenever you decide to get and keep a job to make a living for your family and whenever Barbara can have the respect she deserves from you and her daughter, maybe I will release her. She isn't able to carry the load anymore," the psychiatrist told him.

Don came in with a whole new attitude that evening and brought Sandy with him. Even Sandy appeared to see me in a different light than before. We discussed moving to Barry to be closer to my family so that Don could get a job there and begin to support his family.

A few days later, he came with the good news that he found a job at Barry and we shared it with my doctor. Soon after that, I was released from the hospital with outpatient counseling and counseling with my psychiatrist in Alton as well.

After we moved to Barry, I spent a lot of time sleeping to escape the depression which loomed around me all the time. We made frequent trips to Alton for counseling sessions with my psychiatrist and I attended private counseling sessions at the counseling center near my home. Don finally allowed me to be Sandy's mother, to discipline her as she needed to be, and she began helping me instead of fighting against me. This sudden change of events and hearts played an enormous role in my recovery, although it was still very difficult at times.

After several medication changes had been made during different hospitalizations the depression still was out of control. As a final alternative, my psychiatrist suggested shock treatments. We were reluctant at first but after weighing the facts and my lack of success in overcoming the depression with medications and counseling, we decided to go ahead with them.

I was admitted to a hospital near St. Louis, Missouri for the series of E.C.T. treatments. The identical repeated experiences I had with each of them were amazing but puzzling at the same time. Every time the doctor started the anesthesia, I felt as if I were drowning and immediately heard the roar of ocean waves in my ears. Then, just as I gasped for breath, I had a vision of a man on an air boat who came to rescue me. I never saw his face but he calmly and sweetly said to me, "Come fly with me, and they won't hurt you!" Peacefully I climbed on the seat behind him, put my arms around his waist, and we took off, never touching the water. The next thing I knew I was waking up in my room, completely oriented as to who, where, when, and why I was there, and the staff was shocked. I was told that usually electric shock treatments left patients groggy, disoriented, and sometimes permanently brain damaged. The first couple of times I experienced this vision, I just thought I was going off the deep end so I didn't tell anyone but it happened exactly the same way each time. These shock treatments were very effective and I was so thankful for the relief from the deep dark depression that enveloped me before.

Until a few years ago, I thought it was my guardian angel who rescued me. One morning as I was worshipping and having communion with the Lord, He impressed upon my heart that it was He who had rescued me! Wow! What an honor and privilege to have the Savior of the universe come to my rescue! Tears of joy flooded my eyes and rolled down my cheeks as I thanked Him from the bottom of my heart!

In 1983, after a long drawn out battle for workman's compensation and Social Security Disability as a result of this breakdown, I won the case. When I received my settlement from the State of Illinois we bought a home in Hillview, Don's home town, and remodeled it totally.

One morning in 1984 during a hospital stay for a change of depression medication, my doctor shocked me when he said, "Barbara, I want you to go back to school while you have a steady income and can get some assistance."

"What?" I asked in disbelief. "I can't even remember my own name, much less learn anything new!" I replied.

"Try it and prove to me that you can't and I will accept that," he wisely responded. "I don't think you will ever be able to return to nursing so I want you to get some other training while you can."

After much thought, I decided to try to go to Medical Laboratory Technician School because staying in the medical profession was more comfortable for me. I applied at Lewis and Clark Community College in Godfrey and was accepted right away into their program. The department of Vocational Rehabilitation helped me finance my new schooling. As I neared completion of my first semester there, we had decided to move back to Barry to be closer to my family once again.

During my final examinations at Lewis and Clark, I started having a lot of problems with my stomach and was admitted to the hospital in Pittsfield, Illinois with peptic ulcers. Shortly after my discharge, I had more problems and was admitted to the hospital again with medication induced hepatitis and was extremely ill. For almost three whole days, I didn't know much of anything because I was so sick. It was during this time that I quit smoking and Don did too so it would be easier for me when I got to come home. I was so proud of him for making this sacrifice of love for me.

I excelled in my classes and had a great grade point average. After my prerequisite college classes were completed I enrolled in Blessing Hospital's School of Medical Laboratory Technicians in Quincy, Illinois to finish my training. I graduated in 1986 with an Associate degree, and it was one of the happiest days of my life. My family members attended and were all very proud of me.

I had mailed my psychiatrist a graduation announcement and he planned to close his office that day so he and his wife could come to watch me graduate. But the receptionist misplaced it so they missed my graduation. Dr. Theodoro was very happy for me when I saw him for my next visit. "Barbara, you are one in a million because most people who have a breakdown that severe never recover, much less go on to do anything more with their lives," he said. He surely knew what strings to pull to get me motivated and I was so thankful!

CHAPTER 6
A NEW SEASON

Since there were no openings for a laboratory technician at the time of my graduation, I started working in a nursing home as an L.P.N. until 1987. After medications, exercise, and physical therapy failed to relieve my extreme low back pain, the only alternative left was a lumbar fusion. This was a very risky surgery because if anything went wrong, I could be paralyzed for the rest of my life. Since the back pain was constant and excruciating, I was desperate. I applied for Social Security disability again because I knew that I would be unable to work for at least a year so my case was reopened without a problem. I was so thankful, but the following year proved to be another testing ground for me.

My pride made it very difficult for me to ask for the help I needed from my family because I had always been the caregiver. The first six weeks following the surgery, I had to wear a body cast which extended from just below my bust line all the way down to my hips. It severely limited my mobility, so I had to have a lot of help with bathing, bathroom trips, and everything else I was used to doing on my own. My daughter became my best friend during this time, as well as my most able assistant, even though my husband did his part too. It really felt strange for the ones I had always cared for to be caring for me now. I had to wear a plastic wrap-around brace for the next six months after the body cast was removed, which was very unpleasant and challenging as well.

After being released to go back to work, I finally acquired a position as a lab technician in a hospital. I started my own paramedical business as a second income, because Don's work in the apple orchard was only seasonal. I really enjoyed going to meet new people in their homes with my newfound business. For the next three years I diligently worked two jobs outside the home. However our marriage relationship continued to deteriorate rapidly.

Another unexpected challenge came in 1993, when I had to have another surgery done. As I was in the hospital room recovering from the anesthesia, I was sitting up in my bed sipping tea and trying to eat some Jell-O, when suddenly everything went dark and I passed out. When I woke up I was almost standing on my head in the bed with an IV going full speed and oxygen in my nose. As I looked around me, all of my children and my husband were standing around my bed with teary eyes and concerned looks on their faces.

"What happened?" I questioned.

"You had a reaction to the anesthesia they gave you," replied my husband. "We thought we had lost you for certain this time, Barb," he said squeezing my hand tightly.

One day after I had sufficiently recovered from this surgery, Don asked me to sit down to talk with him. "Barb, I have been thinking about going to Oklahoma to work with my brother Steve. He has offered me some good money and I can stay with him so it won't be a hardship. What do you think? "

"Do you really think that you will be happy there?" I inquired. By this time, our daughter Sandy was married and had two beautiful daughters of her own. I wasn't sure he would want to leave her and our granddaughters in Illinois.

"I can't make any money here to help you out. Maybe we both need a little break anyway and maybe it will be good for our marriage." he replied.

"You are certainly welcome to try that if you want to. I won't try to hold you back if that's what you really want to do," I answered.

He packed up his clothes and whatever he thought he would need and he left for Oklahoma.

I started thinking about my life and was weighing out my desires, hopes, and dreams. I just wasn't happy with anything anymore. Don and I talked over the phone quite a bit and he seemed happy in Oklahoma. He was finally enjoying working. After lengthy discussions, I decided that if I wanted to save my marriage of twenty-five years, I needed to move to Oklahoma to be with him.

One night when he called me I said, "Don, I have been thinking a lot about us lately. Are you planning on staying in Oklahoma now? If you are, why don't I just move out there too and we can work on our marriage? Maybe we can work it all out that way."

After several more serious conversations, he agreed to my suggestion. I went to visit him before we started making solid plans to move. When I returned from that visit, we sold our home to Sandy and her husband and I applied for my Oklahoma nursing license. In January of 1994, we moved our belongings to our new apartment in Shawnee, Oklahoma. After I started working in a nursing home as an L.P.N., things seemed to be going better for us for a little while.

"I'm going to move back to Illinois to be close to Sandy and the grandchildren," Don unexpectedly announced to me one day shortly after that. "You are going with me, aren't you?"

"No, I'm not!" I replied. "I moved here to work on our marriage!" I knew in my heart that I was to stay in Oklahoma for this season of my life and I needed the change. I could see the disappointment in his eyes, but some unknown force held me back.

For the next three years, I made monthly trips to Illinois to visit him and my family but I knew things were changing in both our relationship and our hearts. I couldn't quite decide at that time what it was but something was compelling me to stay in Oklahoma. Soon it became almost impossible for us to communicate. Our love was changing and I knew in my heart that our marriage was over. The only thing we had in common now was our daughter and grandchildren. I could no longer handle the idea of being a "weekend wife". There was nothing left to salvage of the broken pieces of our marriage, so I filed for divorce in January of 1997. I had to get some clear direction for the rest of my life but I had to let go of the past to be able to do it.

CHAPTER 7
THE TURNING POINT

1997 was the beginning of a series of events that changed my whole life completely. After I divorced Don, I met and started dating a man who convinced me to start praying and seeking the Lord again. As it says in the Bible, "God uses the foolish things to confound the wise" (1 Corinthians 1:27 KJV). I met him in a bar one night and I knew immediately that there was something very special about this new friend. Although I had no intention of seeking God through this relationship, I discovered that he knew a whole lot about the Bible and the Lord. After we started dating, he encouraged me to pray and to read my Bible.

We spent hours talking about the Lord, even though I would never listen to my older sister when she tried to discuss these things with me. In the next few months we faced many trials and storms together but we always sought the Lord in all of them. Among my challenges were the loss of my relationships with all three of my children, false accusations at work, and the death of one of my favorite clients who was like a son to me. As a result my physical and emotional health deteriorated rapidly.

Since I was unable to work two jobs, I finally had to take bankruptcy with the loss of my home, car, other possessions, and a growing codependency upon the man I had begun to love deeply. The final blow that totally devastated me was when Darrell ended our relationship in November and I was all alone. My heart was shattered into a million pieces.

Immediately a deep depression enveloped me like a thick cloud and thoughts of suicide invaded my mind continuously as hopelessness and helplessness set in.

"Sandy, I love you so much!" I sobbed as I called my daughter on the telephone with tears streaming down my face.

"Mama, what's wrong now?" I could tell she was overwhelmed with fear because this type of phone call had become a red flag to her over the years as I had struggled with depression and suicide. "Have you done anything to yourself or are you planning to?" she inquired. "What's going on?"

"Darrell just walked out on me and ended our relationship! I just can't make it without him! I have nothing and no one to love me!" I cried out painfully.

"Where is he now?" she asked.

"I think he went to his mother's house but I don't know for sure." I answered.

"What is his mom's telephone number, Mom? I'm going to call him to see if he will take you to the hospital to get you some help! I'm not there and don't know for sure how soon I can be there all the way from Illinois! I don't want you to give him any problem about going to the hospital either, ok?" she said lovingly but sternly. I looked up the phone number for her and got back on the line with her. "Mama, I want you to promise me that you will get a crisis counselor on the telephone with you and stay on there with them until I beep back in again!"

She knew that I couldn't break a promise to her so she felt more reassured when I agreed and proceeded to call the crisis center. She waited until I got connected with the crisis center to call Darrell. Soon she beeped back in on the other line.

"Mom, Darrell is on his way to your house to take you to the hospital now. I'm going to keep on talking to you until he gets there, and I want to talk to him again. I will be catching the next available flight to Oklahoma to be with you," she reassured me.

When Darrell arrived at our place he came in with a look of horror on his face and asked, "Barb, what's going on with you?"

I couldn't talk to him for crying so I handed him the telephone so he and Sandy could talk again. After they had talked a few minutes he hung up the phone and loaded me up in his car to take me to the hospital.

In the emergency room, Darrell sat on a stool near me in a state of shock as I poured out my life story to the admissions counselor. He had no idea of the messed up life I had lived and struggled with so he apologized to me for not helping me deal with my issues. Shortly after that, I was admitted to the psychiatric unit for individual and group counseling.

My daughter Sandy arrived the next day. She and Darrell spent quite a bit of time together before I was released from the hospital and his attitude changed toward me remarkably. Before she left to go back to Illinois, he promised Sandy that he would keep checking on me to be sure I was alright. We agreed to continue our relationship as "just friends" and he would stay with his mother until other arrangements were made.

After a while Darrell and I decided that he would keep our mobile home and I would find a furnished apartment. I started combing the classified ads in the newspaper and finally found one that appealed to me in late December. I called about it and made arrangements to go see it. The landlady and landlord were very wonderful, warm, loving people, and I really liked the apartment. It was a perfect fit for me so I paid my rent and told them I planned to move in on New Year's Day, 1998. Darrell agreed to help me move my heavy furniture in his pickup truck.

I was doing pretty well until New Year's Eve, which was a night we normally would have gone partying together. As the evening progressed some tormenting thoughts in my mind kept asking me *"Where is Darrell?"*, *"Who is he with?"*, and *"What about me?"* Self-pity, depression, and suicidal thoughts engulfed me once again. I started seriously contemplating where I could go to get so drunk I couldn't see. Then I secretly planned to crash my car into something so big I would never survive. My thinking was, *"It will all be over then, and there will be no more pain!"*

Satan thought he had me right where he wanted me but suddenly from out of the blue, I heard a thundering voice saying, *"No, you will go to church tonight!"* I thought surely I had lost my mind and looked around to make sure there was no one else in my mobile home playing tricks on me. There was no one but me and the Lord and in my heart I knew that I had finally heard the voice of God speak to me.

Just the night before, I had been at a friend's home praying with him. Rick had given me a piece of paper with the name and phone number of a church in Moore, Oklahoma by the unction of the Holy Spirit. "If you ever decide to go to church, this one is a good one," he said. I just shrugged it off with my rebellious independent attitude. When I got home, I carelessly threw it down on the end table beside my favorite chair.

It wasn't but a few minutes after I heard that booming voice that my eyes fell onto that piece of paper. I felt a strong urgency to call that church to ask about New Year's Eve services. So I nervously dialed the phone number, not knowing what to expect. It had been twenty-eight years since I had been to church for anything except funerals and weddings, so this was totally out of my comfort zone.

After a couple of rings, a sweet voice answered, "Revival for Christ Club, this is Della. How can I help you?"

"Are you having New Year's Eve Services there tonight?" I inquired shakily.

"No, but we are having fellowship with games, food, fun, and will be praying the old year out and the new one in," she answered. I wasn't at all prepared for the next words I heard from her on the other end of the line.

"Are you Barbara?" she asked.

"How do you know my name?" I asked, intimidated by her question. My name wasn't on the telephone account so I knew she didn't get it from caller ID and it blew my mind that she knew who I was.

"The Lord told us a lady named Barbara would be calling us tonight because she is in desperate need of help. That is you, isn't it?" she asked confidently. This was all too spooky for me and I found myself trembling in fear, with cold chills running all over my body. I was sure I was having a dream or something, so I tried to shake myself awake.

"Barbara, you need to come so we can pray for you and help you!" she continued reassuringly.

"I don't have any decent clothes to wear!" I responded.

"We are wearing sweat shirts and jeans because we aren't in the main sanctuary. We are in the fellowship hall. But it wouldn't matter anyway because God looks at your heart not your clothes! Please come join us, we love you."

I finally agreed and asked for directions to the church so I could write them down. After I took my shower, put on my jeans and a sweat shirt, I grabbed my car keys and headed out to the church. It was as if some invisible force was pushing me all the way and I could not resist.

In my overwhelmed state of mind, I forgot my directions to the church but the next thing I realized, I was sitting in the church parking lot, not even remembering leaving Midwest City. I had never been to Moore, OK before, much less off the interstate on the side streets. It was as if God himself had driven me there. As I opened the door of the car and proceeded to stand up, it was as if my legs both became like Jell-O and I was shaking all over.

"Lord You have brought me here to this place, now give me the strength to walk," I prayed.

As I entered the foyer, I didn't immediately see anyone there so I thought, *"Good, this is my chance to get out of here! I did come to church."*

At that very moment, Della came running out of the fellowship hall, grabbed me, and gave me one of the warmest hugs I had ever experienced. "Barbara, we are so glad you came! Come meet some of our church family!"

"How did you know who I was?" I asked fearfully.

"God showed us a vision of you," she replied with a beautiful smile.

I couldn't imagine God loving me that much. I followed her into the fellowship hall although I felt like a little lost puppy. I was amazed by the warm welcome I received. She introduced me to about thirty of the nicest people I had ever met. Every one of them stood up, gave me a hug, and told me that they loved me. I couldn't understand this because they didn't know me and they certainly didn't know the sinful life I had been living.

"How can you love me when you don't even know me?" I asked in awe. "Because God loves you, we do too!" replied one of the ladies.

I found a seat across the table from a beautiful blonde lady who had a special warm glow about her that I had never seen on anyone. She had sparkling blue eyes that appeared to dance with joy and a precious sweet smile that warmed my heart. We began talking a little bit. It was getting quite noisy in that room so she asked me if I would like to go someplace quiet to talk and pray. As I agreed to go with her she asked if we could take a prayer warrior with us. I asked her what a prayer warrior was and she explained that it was someone who prayed for everyone. The three of us made our way down the hallway to a beautiful, peaceful, little room with some big comfortable chairs to sit in. On the way to the room I determined in my mind, *"I'm not telling them anything! They will only judge me like everyone else always has. I don't want to be condemned again!"*

My attitude was changed in a heartbeat as I sat down across from Alethea, the blonde, as she quietly and sweetly said to me, "Now, Barbara, what's going on in your life that's so bad?"

Suddenly every bit of my nasty life story gushed out as the flood gates were opened by the Lord. All my tormented thoughts and my entire life were suddenly exposed as I wept and sobbed uncontrollably. All the shame and guilt that I had tried so hard to hide were released as I poured out my heart to these ladies. I just couldn't stop it no matter how hard I tried. When I finally got quiet she asked me if we could pray together, so I consented. We stood up, joined hands, and started praying in agreement.

Suddenly I felt like a bolt of lightning surged through my body from my head to my toes, causing me to drop to my knees crying and sobbing uncontrollably once again. I was very frightened since I had no clue what was happening to me, so I cried out, "What was that?"

"Relax, honey, the Lord just touched you", Alethea responded.

"Touched me, He knocked me down!" I retaliated.

"No, He loves you very much and He humbled you," she said sweetly.

I was indeed humbled as my former pride and determination to rebel against releasing all those years of bitterness and anger were dissipated in a moment. I knew without a doubt that I had been encountered by my Heavenly Father who loved me unconditionally. As I continued to cry an ocean of tears, I stayed on my knees and repented of all my sins, asking God to forgive me. As I did, I cried out to Him, "God, either kill me or use me, but get me out of this miserable life!"

At that very moment, in the twinkling of an eye, I felt a two-ton burden lift from my shoulders, and an overwhelming sense of pure love that I had never felt before in my whole life. I fully surrendered my life to Jesus Christ that night, a decision I have never regretted.

We then returned to the fellowship hall where the others celebrated my decision with me and my heart became filled with joy and peace. As we prayed the old year out and the new one in, I gained a sense of confidence knowing that finally my heart was right with my Creator and my life would never be the same again!

CHAPTER 8
A SECOND CHANCE

As I awakened New Year's Day early in the morning, I had a new joy and a song of praise to the Lord in my heart that just wouldn't quit. "Thank You, Lord, for saving my soul and for my new life with You!" With a supernatural burst of energy that I hadn't experienced in years and a big smile on my face, I started packing my belongings. By the time Darrell got there to help me move my heavy things, I had already packed most of my things and even moved a couple of loads to the apartment in our Camaro.

"What did you do last night? Where did you get all this energy? Why do you keep smiling and singing?" he asked in amazement as he watched me joyfully flitting about.

"I went to church and gave my life to Jesus!" I responded with the biggest smile I can ever remember having on my face.

He suddenly got very quiet. I could tell that he was happy for me and amazed at the immediate transformation he saw in me.

The darkness in my life was lifted and I felt a glow all around me like the one I had seen on Alethea the night before. After we finished moving my things to my new apartment Darrell went home, still shocked by my unusual New Year's Eve celebration.

I prayed and dedicated my new apartment to the Lord and His

work, covering it in the blood of Jesus and anointing it with oil. I was so overwhelmed with God's love and presence that I sang and danced around like a child as I transformed our apartment into a home. The fireplace mantle in my living room quickly became my own private altar for the Lord and the stained glass windows in the kitchen made it feel even more like the Lord's home.

As I returned to work at the orthopedic clinic the next day, I caught many glances from my coworkers as they noticed the drastic changes in my demeanor and even my walk. I had pep in my step, a smile on my face, and joy in my heart. They had never seen this in me before so I knew they were trying to figure out what had happened to me.

"What happened to you, Barbara?" my director of nursing inquired. "You look so different and so happy!" she said.

"I gave my life to Jesus Christ on New Year's Eve!" I exclaimed with tears of joy rolling down my cheeks. She was excited but intrigued because the transformation in me was undisputable and astounding. During my recent crises, it was with her compassionate listening ear and wisdom from the Lord that she had been able to encourage me in the past few months.

"God set me free from depression on New Year's Eve when I gave my life to Jesus Christ!" I proudly announced to my mental health counselor when I followed up with her. I was overjoyed as I shared the great news of my transformation with her. Unfortunately, she didn't share my views that my mental health was remarkably improved by my "salvation". She expected me to keep returning with all my problems but I knew in my heart that God had delivered me. "I won't be back to see you anymore because I don't need counseling now!" I happily announced. She gave me a skeptical glance as I left the office.

In the next few months my landlady Hazel and I spent many hours together talking about the Lord. I felt as if she and her husband Harold had adopted me as their own child. I was so hungry and thirsty for God's Word that I couldn't get enough prayer, church, TV ministry, or reading my Bible. Praise and worship music constantly permeated the air in our home and I spent many hours just basking in the presence of the Lord. I was growing spiritually by leaps and bounds as the Lord took me through some much needed deliverance and healing - physically, emotionally, and spiritually.

As I continued to attend the church where I surrendered, I quickly grew in my walk with the Lord as I studied the Word of God and enjoyed the fellowship and the presence of the Lord. Every time I went was exciting because I went with expectancy in my heart that something good was going to happen that day and it always did. I started gaining confidence, knowing that I was a child of the Most High God and started coming out of my shell being friendlier while reaching out to others. As I started learning the scriptures and speaking them out loud over my life I could see changes for the better. Through the church God brought me new family and friends and a whole new outlook on life.

One evening during worship, my eyes fell on a lady in the congregation who was surrounded by a dark cloud of depression, (which I quickly recognized), as she cried out to God. As I obeyed the Holy Spirit and wrapped my arms around her, we cried together as the Lord poured out His love on both of us. I knew in my heart that Wanda was a divine connection as a part of God's plan. He had strategically placed us together here for such a time as this. After church, we talked a while, and I listened as she poured out her heart to me. Wanda and I became best friends and spent a lot of time together praying and having fellowship with the Lord.

I called all three of my children, bubbling over with joy as I told them about my salvation and the changes in my life. Their reactions weren't what I had hoped for though. They were so familiar with the old Barbara and my past, that they were skeptical. My family members back home in Illinois thought that the marked changes were temporary and that maybe I had "gotten involved in a cult" or "gone off the deep end". The sudden radical changes in me were too obvious for most of them to understand.

Frustration set in as I sensed their lack of faith that these changes would last. As I learned the authority Jesus had given me over the lies of the enemy, I stood on the Word of God and refused to be moved by people's reactions to what I knew in my heart had taken place. It wasn't easy but the Lord gave me the grace and courage to endure the persecution.

I invited my sons to come visit me in my new apartment so we could try to renew and restore our relationships. Nick, my oldest son, was the first to come see me. He and Christa, my daughter-in-law, came by one day and were happy that I had a new apartment and was no longer living with Darrell. They really didn't want to hear much of my experience of salvation since they weren't living for God, but at least they had come by.

"Son, will you please forgive me for all the pain I have caused you in your life?" I asked. He was very shocked and surprised. I sensed his pain was very deep and knew it would take a while for him to forgive me, but at least I had admitted to him and to myself how much I had hurt him and told him I was sorry. They didn't stay long after that.

My youngest son Danny and his wife Tia came by another day to see my apartment. Danny sat down in the living room across from me. I could sense that he was mesmerized by the changes that were so apparent but Tia kept trying to distract him. Wanda was sitting on the couch quietly praying in her heart that his attention wouldn't be distracted. As we sat there I shared my salvation experience with him.

In the spirit, I could tell that something had touched his heart. I was sure that the Holy Spirit was working on him.

"Danny, will you please forgive me for not being there for you while you were growing up, and for not being the mom you needed me to be?" I asked boldly.

"Yes, Mom, I do forgive you! I love you!" he replied with tears in his eyes. I was so thankful that Wanda's prayers had been answered and he had been able to keep his focus on what I was saying.

The next few months were what I call "Holy Ghost Boot Camp". I just couldn't get enough of the Lord, His Word, or worship Him enough for who He is and what He had done in my life. As I grew in the Word and my personal relationship with Him, He began to deal with me on the issues in my life that I hadn't confronted such as anger, unforgiveness, bitterness, resentment, jealousy, self-pity, and a host of others. It hurt my feelings to be corrected by Him so much and there were times when I felt like I couldn't please Him or do anything right. But He gently loved me and helped me with each painful deliverance and when it was over, I experienced amazing peace and joy. He constantly reminded me of the scripture that says "Whom the Lord loves He chastises", and He impressed upon me that He was preparing me for a much better life.

The year 1998 was filled with trials and tribulations after I accepted Jesus Christ as the Lord of my life. Sometimes it was very hard to understand why I had to go through so much. It didn't take very long to realize that since I wasn't serving the devil anymore, he was angry and was coming against me with everything he had to try to keep me from pursuing God. Once I understood that, God started helping me become a prayer warrior against the evil works of the enemy. As I started each day, I learned quickly to put on the full armor of God that Ephesians 6:10-18 talks about in the Bible. I almost always spent at least two hours each day praying, worshipping, and reading the Word before I started my day.

Toward the middle of October 1998 early one Sunday morning, as was my custom, I went to do my laundry at the laundromat before church. I carried my clothes inside in my baskets and placed them in front of the washers. As I transferred my clothes into the washers, I noticed a man watching me from the chair where he was sitting. After I started my laundry, I went to sit beside him and started talking with him.

"Hi, I'm Barbara. What is your name?" I asked.

"My name is Mike. I have been working in Florida but I grew tired of being there so I decided to go to Arizona to get a job. As I was traveling toward Arizona, I felt led to come to Oklahoma City instead. Just outside of the city a few miles, my truck broke down. It wasn't worth fixing, so I sold it to a salvage yard and hitchhiked into Oklahoma City where I found my way to the Jesus House, a shelter for the homeless." As I sat there listening to his story, I felt a strange connection to him that I hadn't ever experienced before. My heart ached for him as I felt his pain and the frustration of not knowing the future.

"Do you know Jesus or go to church anyplace?" I asked boldly.

"I have accepted Jesus Christ as my Lord, but I'm not going to church anyplace right now," he replied reluctantly.

"Would you like to go with me to my church this morning?" I asked without even thinking about it.

"Sure, I would like to very much! I love God." he quickly and joyfully replied, accepting my offer.

We both finished our laundry at the same time as we talked together while we folded our clothes.

"May I give you a ride to where you are staying?"

"Uh, no. Please just drop me off at the McDonalds restaurant and pick me up there when you get ready for church. I was working the day I was supposed to have a TB test at the Jesus House so they won't let me come back."

The Lord prompted me to take him back to my apartment until I got ready for church. I was a little hesitant but knew in my childlike faith that the Lord wouldn't ask me to do anything that would harm me so I quickly invited him.

"Are you sure you want to do that?" he inquired. I assured him that the Lord had been the One who put this in my heart. We had coffee together and talked a lot about our different experiences with the Lord. After I got ready for church and came out of my bedroom he smiled and said to me, "You are the most beautiful woman I have ever seen! I know you are going to be my wife!" I just kind of blew this off as a "man thing" but I couldn't help but wonder about it.

We headed out on our journey to the church and enjoyed just getting to know one another better. When we got there I introduced him and asked my church family to pray for Mike for a steady job and a place to live. So we all agreed in prayer for the Lord to move for him in these situations. Worship was really special that day and we were both "slain in the spirit together" as we each sought the Lord with all our hearts. The message was a "head-on" for both of us. After the Word was preached, I took him up to the altar for the pastor to pray for him. She prayed first for me and then for him, and we both were "slain in the spirit". The Lord gave him an awesome word of encouragement but I never got to hear it because it was for his ears only. He never really shared it with me but I saw he was very much encouraged. That afternoon we went back to my apartment, ate some lunch, and went to the flea markets together to enjoy fellowship and the day before our evening church services. I was amazed at how many of the same things we liked and were interested in and how comfortable I was with him. It was a genuine fit, like two pieces of a puzzle coming together. I prayed secretly for wisdom and that God would direct my path with Mike and not let me get my emotions involved because my desire was to be led by the Holy Spirit.

Little did I know that for the next three weeks, Mike would be camping out on the sofa in my apartment. He got a job in the city and worked every day. Whenever I got home from work each day, he helped me to get comfortable by propping my feet up on the couch, and then he prepared our evening meal. After sharing our day with one another over our delicious warm meal, he washed the dishes, and then came in to join me in the living room. He definitely was very different from anyone I had ever known before, and I enjoyed being pampered and made to feel like a queen. We quickly fell in love and in our hearts we both knew that we were meant to be together. He drew a picture one day as a special gift from him to me but wouldn't let me even sneak a peek until it was finished. When I finally did get to see it, it took my breath away and I knew spiritually it was filled with meaning. It was the cross with a beautiful ivy vine wrapped around it with two miniature roses on the vine and there were two white doves above the cross. Wanda interpreted that picture for me later on and even though I don't remember the full meaning, it confirmed our relationship with each other and with the Lord.

Mike had come into my life just as another dark cloud loomed on the horizon. I had a whiplash injury in 1994, shortly after moving to Oklahoma, resulting from an automobile accident. I was experiencing severe pain in my neck and right shoulder, which was not relieved with physical therapy or pain medications. The problems with my cervical spine now needed to be repaired surgically with a fusion of the vertebrae. After scheduling my surgery I called my daughter Sandy to let her know. She and her husband Bill drove to Oklahoma from Illinois to be with me for the surgery. Upon arrival they both immediately loved Mike and readily accepted him as part of our family.

As I went into surgery I had great peace knowing that God was in control and that everything would be all right. After I was taken to the recovery room and my condition was stable, Sandy and Bill headed back to Illinois but Mike remained at my side.

A couple of days later, he came in to visit and brought me a soft, black, stuffed monkey to cuddle. "Honey, my farm in Minnesota has sold so I have to go back there to sign the papers. I will be back by the weekend," he reassured me.

"I will ask my friend Georgia from Shawnee to come get me and take me home when I am discharged from the hospital." With tears in both our eyes, he kissed me goodbye tenderly and left. Mike had taken my car home when I had my surgery. Georgia gave me a lecture about letting a stranger have my car keys but I reassured her that God had prompted me to let him take it home for me and I knew that it would be in the driveway. When she took me home the next day we found my car in the drive, full of gasoline, and the keys were in our secret hiding place.

Darrell, Wanda, and another friend Barbara from our church all came to visit often. Wanda and Barbara helped me to take care of my personal and housekeeping needs. God provided caregivers in every area of my life but I longed for the arms of the man I loved. To this day I have never heard from Mike again but I am so thankful to the Lord for those short three weeks of heaven on earth. The day that I was scheduled to go back to the doctor to be released to go back to work from my surgery, I was so sick that I couldn't get out of bed. So I called his office to reschedule my appointment. After New Year's Day was the earliest one I could get so I called my boss to let her know. She assured me that would be all right since I had let her know what was going on.

When the doctor released me to go back to work, I called my boss again to let her know when I would be in. "I'm sorry, Barbara, the clinic has terminated you because you didn't return to work as you had agreed," she responded.

I couldn't believe what she was telling me. I was devastated by the news. "I called you and explained the situation about my appointment and you assured me that everything would be alright! This means that I have no income and no insurance that I desperately need to get my many prescriptions filled," I responded with tears streaming down my cheeks.

Immediately I started praying desperately, "God, if You really are the God that heals, like I have been taught, please heal and deliver me from all these sicknesses and this depression that keep me in bondage to the medications I have been taking! Being a single person, there is no way I can get help paying for my prescription medications."

In the next few weeks that prayer was amazingly but slowly answered. As I ran out of each medication, I cast my cares upon Him and asked Him to heal me, and He did. Soon, I was off of all of the prescription medications I had taken for years with no withdrawals whatsoever! God had healed me completely just as I had asked Him to! He had also proven to me, that indeed, He still does miracle healings. Hallelujah!

I tried to work something out with the finance company so that I could keep my car but they refused to work with me in any way. I cried out, "God please help me have the grace and strength to let it go because I believe this car was a gift from You!" The day before Christmas they arrived to repossess the car and the peace I had as they pulled it out of the driveway was overwhelming.

Christmas was very lean that year with no gifts under the tree and very little food in my cabinets. Nevertheless it was one of the best Christmases I have ever had. Wanda and I worked together, using what we had and we made an amazing gourmet dinner for Darrell, her, and me. The three of us spent that wonderful Christmas day sharing the love of God while giving Him praise and worship for all the wonderful blessings in our lives.

CHAPTER 9
HUMBLE BEGINNINGS

"Lord, You know the mess my life is in now so I am totally dependent upon You for all my needs!

I am still undergoing medical treatment for that repetitive motion injury to my right shoulder, which I sustained from working at the clinic that fired me. I can't work right now, so what am I to do?" I inquired of the Lord. After waiting a short time, I received the answer and sought an attorney to start proceedings for a workman's compensation claim for this injury.

I knew it would take a while to get my weekly compensation started so I went to talk to my landlady about my rent and my situation. "Hazel, I can't pay my rent for a while now because I am waiting for my workman's compensation to get started. Would you be willing to take a little bit at a time until I get back on my feet and go back to work?" I asked.

"Of course, Barbara, You just pay whatever you can whenever you can and it will be fine!" she replied. "We know that you will pay it whenever you get it and we can trust you to do what you say you will do."

Neither physical therapy nor pain medications eased my right shoulder pain, so I underwent surgery for it in April of 1999. "Darrell and I are here for you, Barb, for whatever you need after your surgery,"

Wanda said. "Just let us know." God had proven Himself faithful once again by providing great friends to help me out in my time of need! Wanda helped me with personal care and dressing changes, and Darrell ran errands for me until I got strong enough to walk.

When I had regained my strength, I got plenty of exercise walking nearly everywhere I had to go that wasn't too far. When my shoulder had healed enough to start driving again I prayed, "Lord, please help me to find another vehicle so I can search for a new job after my release from the doctor."

One day as I was combing the classified ads in the local paper, one of the "For Sale" ads caught my attention. It listed a 1975 Plymouth, the only one priced in my range, so I called the automobile dealer to inquire about it. "I am looking for a dependable vehicle, but I don't have much money right now because I am receiving workman's compensation. Would you work with me on a vehicle if I come out to test drive one? I will have to take a cab to your dealership though," I explained.

"Come on out. We will put you in something and will work out payments you can afford." Victor replied.

I was elated that I was going to have wheels again! The dealership made a few repairs to the car as I waited. After test driving the 1975 Plymouth, we signed the paperwork which included a small weekly payment. I was on my way. The independence of having my own vehicle again really felt great. My old but "new to me" car got me home safely that day.

Nearly every day after that, though, when I ventured away from my apartment I found myself stranded someplace. "Victor, please come rescue me again," was my plea every time I called the dealership.

"Where are you this time?" he would jokingly respond. They made so many repairs that I thought surely it must have everything fixed that it could possibly need. Rarely did they charge me anything. The guys at the dealership were becoming "my new family" that God had chosen to bless me with but little did I know how much He was ministering to them and to me through this situation.

When I was released to go back to work, I prayed, "Father God, please lead me and guide me to the right job that you have for me." I started looking for another L.P.N. position and God opened the door for a position at the women's correctional facility in McCloud, OK. I had finally caught up on my rent with Hazel, but because it was such a long way to drive to work, I started looking for a closer place to live. By God's guidance and direction, I found a small camping trailer in the trailer park where I used to live in Shawnee and rented it. It was tiny but at least it was a roof over my head and something I could afford.

I often laugh when I think back to the day I moved in and heard the Lord say to me, "Welcome to your new humble beginnings!" That is definitely what it was - a very humbling experience - but one for which I am very thankful. God was teaching me that there was a huge difference between needs and wants and that my material possessions and my pride actually meant very little. It was Him meeting my every need and opening my eyes to His definition of true prosperity. Allowing God to strip me of my independent, prideful spirit, and having to lean on Him for everything was a very difficult but wonderful lesson for me. He gave me creative ideas as to how to fix up our little home into a beautiful dwelling place.

"Lord, I hereby dedicate our new home and our car to You and Your service," I prayed.

When I finally received my workman's compensation settlement, I asked the Lord, "Father, may I please get a more dependable vehicle out of this settlement?" The affirmative answer came quickly.

I called Victor about getting me a more dependable vehicle. "What kind of vehicle are you looking for?" he inquired. After I told him I really wanted another Nissan he said, "I have a personal friend at the Nissan Dealer in Midwest City. Would you want me to contact him to make arrangements to purchase one for cash?"

"I would very much appreciate it," I replied.

"Barb, I have found just the right vehicle for you and have made arrangements to purchase it for you," Victor said excitedly whenever he called me soon after. "I know you are going to like this one!"

The day I went to Victor's dealership to pick it up he told me, "I think the Lord was trying to tell me all along that you needed a better car." We took pictures of all of us in my "dealership family" standing beside my new car as a remembrance of the way God had put us together to help one another. This is confirmation to me of the Scripture that says, "Whatever the enemy means for bad, God will use for the good of those who love Him and are called according to His purpose." He had used my lack of funds and the trials we all went through during this time to draw us closer together and to minister to all of us. God had made us a "family" whose ties will never be broken.

"I am getting so tired of the unfair politics of the system here," I said to one of my coworkers after a few months at the prison. "Do you know of any other L.P.N. positions?"

"I work part-time in McCloud at a doctor's office. They are looking for a laboratory technician," my coworker replied.

"Well, guess what! I am a medical laboratory technician! I don't think this is a coincidence!" I replied with joy in my heart.

I believed this was set up by the Holy Spirit so I applied for the position and was hired almost immediately. Although it was less money than I made at the prison, the hours and the atmosphere were much better and conducive to walking in the Spirit of the Lord. My boss, the doctor, was also a "Spirit filled Christian" so we connected quickly. I was a kind of "all areas person", getting to do a little nursing, lab, x-rays, therapy, and receptionist duties too. This position was a gift from God, as all of us in this small clinic were soon established as a "family", and we loved one another. I didn't mind going to work at all because I was really comfortable with these gals, and for the most part, they understood who I was and what I was all about.

In early 2000, as I listened to these ladies talk about their families and husbands, I started feeling the pain of loneliness. "Lord, You know my heart and my innermost thoughts. I am so lonely and could really use a companion to even just go out to have supper with or to a movie occasionally. I know You are all I really need but it would be nice to share some good times with someone special." As I continued to seek the Lord's will in this area, I signed up to join Equally Yoked Christian Singles in Oklahoma City.

Their calendar of events was amazing but there was one particular event that stood out and leaped off the page at me: "Poetry Reading by Candlelight." *"What an interesting idea,"* I thought, as a spark lit up my heart. "Why do I have this sudden interest in poetry since I haven't ever cared that much for poetry? The only poetry I have ever written or read was in my school years," I inquired of the Lord. "Why can't I shake off this desire to attend that event?" We were invited to share our favorite poems with the group. So I thought to myself, *"I will take one with me that someone has sent me via e-mail on the Internet."*

The morning of the event I planned to go straight to the meeting after work. When I tried to print out the poem to take with me, much to my dismay, I couldn't even pull it up. I immediately became angry and whined to the Lord, "I want that poem, Lord! Please help me get it!"

Just as soon as the words came out of my mouth, conviction hit me and I knew that I had been out of line with the Lord by using a tone of voice that I never meant to use. I quickly repented when I heard

Him say, "Excuse Me, you will have what you need." I felt really bad for that moment of letting my flesh dictate my reaction and continued asking Him to forgive me.

The pace at work that day was fairly slow so I prayed. Every few minutes the Lord dropped a word into my spirit to write down on a piece of paper. By lunch time, I had five pairs of rhyming words and I knew that He was up to something. After everyone else had left for lunch, I sat down to bless my lunch. As I prayed over my lunch, I heard in my spirit, "Go get a tablet of paper and a pen." As I obeyed and listened, the Holy Spirit poured out a beautiful poem on that pad which was my testimony of "The Night I Gave my Life to Jesus". By the end of my lunch hour, I had the whole thing and it was almost word for word the way it happened that memorable night. I was shocked and astounded by the way the words had flowed out without any effort on my part, at the clarity of every word, and the vision within the poem. I was so excited at what the Lord had done. I had to share it with everyone in the office and they were all amazed too. Wow! What a precious gift! Little did I know then just how much the Lord would be using that gift to bless others and me.

When it came my turn to share at the singles meeting that night, I read my new poem out loud as chills went all over my body and I felt the awesome presence of God. As I looked around the room, there wasn't even one dry eye. I knew that God did this for a special reason, to touch every heart in that room with His love, including my own.

A couple of weeks later my Aunt Naomi, who lived in Illinois, went home to be with the Lord so I made the trip back to attend her funeral. As I traveled the highways, singing worship and praise to the Lord, I felt His love pouring out on me like a mighty river. I knew He was preparing me for something great. When I arrived at my daughter's home, I felt led to get a tablet and pen right away. Right there at her dining room table, even before we got a chance to visit much, He poured out a poem to me in remembrance of my Aunt Naomi who had been a real prayer warrior. Mom came in before I got done writing the poem, so she sat down questioningly gazing at the way the words were flowing onto the paper. "Hi Mom, I have a poem we need to share with the pastor performing the service," I said as I finished writing.

"Is this going to get me in trouble?" she asked.

"No, Mom, God is behind this and everything will be all right." After this reassurance, she took me to the pastor's home and introduced me as her daughter from Oklahoma. I explained to Carla, the pastor that the Lord had given me this poem in honor of Aunt Naomi and I believed He wanted her to share it with the family at the service.

As she read it, the tears started welling up in her eyes. "This poem must be read at her service, even though everything has already been planned," she said.

I took the poem back to Sandy's home and was going to type it up when the Lord started ministering another poem to me. This new poem was one of blessings to the minister for being obedient to God to read Aunt Naomi's poem at her service. That weekend I must have written at least ten different poems for loved ones to encourage them and bring them peace. Aunt Naomi's home-going service was very anointed and blessed as the presence and comfort of God surrounded us all. I read aloud her tribute and a special poem for her grandchildren that the Lord had given to me, as the Lord poured out His love upon us.

After that, nearly every holiday, special event, and trial, the Lord gave me a poem of encouragement. This was one gift that I had never asked for but a beautiful everlasting gift that I could use to glorify Him the rest of my life. I soon realized that it is much more precious than gold and I still use it to encourage and uplift people. Staying humble and realizing that without Him I can't do it is very important, so I am careful to always give Him the glory and honor. I now know that all this is part of His prosperity because my soul prospers with this gift too!

CHAPTER 10
LEARNING TO TRUST GOD

The next two years were filled with learning experiences, both good and bad, as the Lord taught me to truly trust Him. Even though I never found my life mate through Equally Yoked, I made some very special connections with two other single ladies that lasted for many years. Jean was an older lady I met at one of the events and she became my closest prayer partner.

One evening the Lord led me to my neighbor's home to meet his sister. "Barb, this is Debbie.

She is looking for new friends and I told her that you are single and would probably enjoy having her for a friend too."

"It is so nice to meet you!" I responded. After a little while of chatting with her I said, "How would you like to go with me to Oklahoma City this weekend for an event at Equally Yoked Christian Singles? It is a really nice group of people and we have a lot of fun getting to know one another. We have food, prayer, bible study, and fellowship."

"That sounds like it would be a lot of fun. I think I will," she responded.

It was an immediate "God connection", and soon we became best friends. We went to church together and spent great fellowship time together with the Lord.

My continued friendship with Darrell opened up doors for more divine connections with other believers who he knew as well.

When God spoke to my heart that my season was over at the Revival for Christ Club church where I had received my salvation, God strategically placed me in another church near Oklahoma City called Church of the Harvest. Although it was a thirty-five mile drive one way, it was worth every mile and every moment it took to get there. This church was larger than the first one but they had a lot more opportunities to learn and grow. Debbie and I signed up for the Winning Women program taught by Pastor Nancy, the senior pastor's wife. This program helped us to learn what our mission in life is and helped us know a lot more about our spiritual being within us. It was amazing how the Lord opened our eyes to the callings He has on our lives. He also brought us new revelations of truth from the scriptures.

As I sat under these eye-opening teachings of the Word of God, the Lord started dealing with me about tithing and giving offerings. I was struggling from paycheck to paycheck, barely having enough to get by and rarely having enough money to pay the bills. I had heard teaching on tithing and giving in the other church but I had reasoned my way out of tithing. "God, if I give a tenth of my money to You, I can't possibly pay the bills and I don't think that will please You!" I reasoned.

As I learned more about giving the conviction became stronger. One night in desperation, while in prayer, I heard the Lord say to me, "Test Me in this and see if I don't open up the windows of heaven and pour you out blessings you can't even contain!" (Malachi 3:10).

At the next church service, I finally listened and obeyed. Although it was like pulling teeth, I gave that tenth of my gross income in the offering plate that day. I was tired of the Lord dealing with me and thought to myself, *"If it doesn't work, I don't have to do it again."* I breathed a sigh of relief as I felt the Lord release me for obeying and trusting Him.

The next two weeks God supernaturally provided for all my needs and all my payments were made. I was shocked and astounded at the way everything fell into place. There was no way my human mind could comprehend the way this worked out, because on paper it just didn't balance out. I'm not going to say it was easy to always give the tithe after that but the Lord had proven to me that He is my source and my provider, and all I needed to do was trust and obey. I had now moved into a powerful new level of faith in my walk with God. My blessings, peace, and hope increased as I continued to give my tithe faithfully. It wasn't long until I began giving offerings over and above the tithe, which opened the door for more abundant blessings from the Lord.

Shortly after I started tithing, the Lord blessed me with a better paying position at Deaconess Hospital in Oklahoma City. I went to visit Hazel and Harold, my former landlords, to see if they had any empty apartments I could rent. "Of course we do for you, Barbara! We are so happy you are back!" Hazel answered.

I moved into a ground floor apartment in the house next door to where I had lived right after my salvation. Soon my second son Danny and his girlfriend Traci moved in upstairs next door to me. A short time later, the Lord opened the door for Debbie a new job in Oklahoma City and she moved into an apartment across the hall from me. Danny and Traci started going to church with Deb and me from time to time, and we often ate our evening meals together as a family.

"Danny and Traci are going to church with me tonight to watch 'Heavens Gates, Hells Flames'," Deb announced to me one day. That was a live play at church they were performing for just a few days. I had to work that evening so I couldn't go but I was thrilled to hear that they were going with her. We had been praying for their salvation and deliverance.

"We gave our lives to Jesus last night, Mom," Traci announced proudly the next day. What an awesome blessing it was to know that they were saved now! God was restoring what the enemy had stolen from me in a mighty way.

Satan didn't like what God was doing here, so Debbie and I prayed daily against the spiritual warfare that had increased remarkably.

My car started having transmission problems which would cost more to fix than I could afford. "Father God, in the precious name of Jesus, I come humbly before Your throne of grace and I ask You to intervene in my transportation situation. I thank You now that You have heard my prayer, and You will answer in your time and your way," I prayed.

My prayer was answered unexpectedly one memorable day after I got home from working the night shift. God led me to the Nissan dealer in Midwest City to see what they had. As I was cruising through the parking lot admiring the new Nissans a young man came out to meet me. "Can I help you with something?" he asked courteously.

"I am looking for a late model Nissan, preferably a Sentra," I responded. He took me to a brand new one on the lot to test drive. It was a gray Nissan Sentra and it seemed like the perfect fit for me.

When we got back to the dealership I parked it in front of the showroom window.

"Let's go in and see what we can do to get you into this car today," he said. I have to admit, I had a lot of doubt since it had only been four years since I had filed bankruptcy, so I really couldn't see how this would work out for me. I knew that God had led me there this particular day for a reason.

Before we went inside to make a deal, the Lord impressed upon me to ask if they had a gold car like this one.

When I asked God why in my heart, the Lord said, "I am refining you as pure gold, and I want you to have the gold one."

Smiling, I looked at the salesman and asked, "Do you have a gold car just like this one?"

He looked shocked as he replied, "Yes, as a matter of fact, it was just unloaded off the truck here yesterday! Why?"

"The Lord wants me to have the gold one," I replied with a huge smile on my face and a twinkle in my eyes.

He didn't question me about this even though he had that certain look on his face like "Really?" He drove the gray Nissan back to the lot where it was before and brought up the gold one, parking it in front of the showroom window.

After admiring it for a few minutes we went inside and proceeded with the paperwork. I struggled a little bit when he came back with the figures of the trade, especially with the payment figure of over four-hundred dollars per month. My fear and hesitation was because I had already lost three cars to repossession and I didn't want to go through that again.

I prayed in my heart, "Lord, that payment is ridiculously high! How am I going to do this?"

In His still quiet reassuring voice in my heart I heard the Lord say to me, "You will not lose this car! I will make a way where there seems to be no way."

"Well, let's go for it!" was my bold statement then to the salesman. Suddenly he had a great big smile on his face that lit up in his countenance.

After the paperwork was signed this young salesman said, "Yours is my first sale here at this dealership!" Now my eyes were opened to the fact that God had also made this car sale an opportunity for me to share with him about the Lord. He had seen with his own eyes how the Lord worked out an impossible situation in my favor because I loved the Lord with all my heart and finally trusted Him. Two hours after I had pulled out of my driveway at my apartment to go find a vehicle, I drove back in with my new car. Wow, this was amazing! Everyone was shocked and surprised when they heard my testimony of how the Lord worked in my life. It was a great witness to them, too.

God's timing was perfect, as always, because Deb and I wanted to go to Missouri to a Christian retreat that weekend. The retreat was held by Disciples Fellowship International, the organization that Mike and Karen, my missionary friends, had founded. We made the trip in comfort without fear of the car breaking down, praising and worshipping God all the way for who He was and what He was doing in our lives.

Following the praise and worship that evening at the retreat, the guest pastor from St. Louis, Mo, who we had never met before, stopped in the middle of his message. He called Deb and me to the altar to give us a Rhema word from the Lord. "I see each of you in your own apartment desperately crying out for the Lord to intervene in your situations. He knows your needs and desires and He is going to answer your prayers. Don't give up, but keep pressing into the Word and to the Lord, and watch to see what He will do for you!" he said.

The words God spoke to us through this willing vessel were incredibly encouraging, and we both knew that this meeting was a divine appointment. We returned home with our hearts and minds full of joy and peace knowing that God was in control of our lives and He would meet our every need.

A week to the day from when I got my new car, the Lord blessed Deb the same way with a new Nissan pickup truck. The same salesman I had for my new car also made the deal with her for her pickup. It was totally amazing!

"Why don't you come out to visit us?" my friend Wanda asked when I was talking to her on the phone one day. She had moved back to Utah where she had come from a few years earlier. The Lord had blessed her with a new husband there.

"I would love to but I don't have the money to make a round trip to Utah," I replied.

"If you can get here, I will make sure you have enough to get back to Oklahoma," she replied.

The Lord had been ministering to me about a new beginning because the spiritual warfare against me in Oklahoma City had recently increased so greatly. When Wanda invited me to come visit her, I knew in my heart that God was getting ready to relocate me and I sensed that it was in Utah. I was excited, yet reluctant at the same time, because that was so far away from my family. As I continued to pray about this trip, the Lord encouraged me to prepare my resume, references, and my spirit for the soon coming changes. I just kept hearing *"New beginning"* in my spirit.

"Wanda, I am calling to accept your invitation for a visit. When would be the best time for me to come out?" After praying together for God's timing, we decided on August of 2001.

When the day for me to leave on my vacation trip finally arrived, I loaded up my little 2001 Nissan and headed down the road on my long journey to Utah. I cranked up my stereo with praise and worship music and prayed as the Lord and I traveled down the road together. I didn't have the money to stay in motels so I drove until I got tired, then pulled over in a rest area. I locked my doors, prayed for protection, curled up in the back seat, and snoozed peacefully in the arms of Jesus. It took me two days and a night of driving to get there. I was elated when I got to Riverton, Utah. I had spent the last of my cash a couple of hundred miles back and I reached the service station in Riverton just in time because the gas gauge was on empty.

I went inside to call Wanda and a few minutes later she came to lead me to her home. Walt was at work when I got there so this gave us an opportunity to catch up a little bit before he came home. "It is so good to see you, and even more wonderful to see you happy and blessed!" I said to her. "The Lord has been ministering to me about moving out here so I have come prepared to find a job while I am here." She was very excited about this news and she shared their plans to take me to the southern part of Utah on some sight-seeing adventures while I was there, including the Grand Canyon. I had never been there before but I had heard about how beautiful it is.

The next morning I got up early to pray and read my Bible. "God if it is Your will that I move out here, please open the door for that new job today before we leave," I prayed.

Soon Wanda stumbled sleepily out to the kitchen where I was drinking my coffee. "What's going on, Sis?" she asked. "The Lord woke me up and told me to come talk to you."

I smiled back at her and replied confidently, "The Lord is going to show you where I need to go to apply for work." Then I proceeded to the bathroom to apply my makeup and get dressed.

A few minutes later she exclaimed, "HealthSouth Rehabilitation Hospital."

She got dressed and within an hour we were on our way to the hospital where I asked for an application for employment. Once completed, I turned it in to the human resources director, who called the director of nursing. Smoothly, just like all God's definite plans seem to go, the door opened for me to have an interview after just a few minutes. Within two hours of my arrival at the hospital, my references were checked, background check completed, drug screen done, and the job was mine with an hourly rate higher than I had ever made before. Just thinking about the way it all fell into place so quickly sent my mind into a frenzy. With a confidence that only God could give me,

I told the director of nursing, "I will see you in about three weeks to start my new job."

"I doubt that you will have your Utah license that quickly. It usually takes at least six weeks for an out of state nurse to receive her nursing license."

Our vacation tour was wonderful and I stood in pure awe of God, especially when I stood on an outlook at the Grand Canyon and admired the beauty He had created. There were many other beautiful sights and we enjoyed being together again very much.

When it was time to go back to Oklahoma, Wanda gave me the money to get back home. "I will have my nursing license sent to your address if it is all right with you because it will speed up the process." She agreed that it would be fine with her. After arriving back home, I wrote my resignation notice and started completing the forms to obtain my Utah nursing license, praying for God's favor. I was excited about my new beginning, but it was most of all to get away from the spiritual warfare I was battling continuously.

"Deb, if I give you gas money, will you please help me move my things to Utah?" I asked. She reluctantly agreed so we asked my sons' step-brother Paul to go with us to help her drive back.

I planned to leave on September 12, 2001, so I was packing on September 11 when the news flash came on television about the planes crashing into the twin towers in New York City. Shocked at this news, a little fear crept in when I heard stories of how there would be an immediate shortage of gasoline. I started crying out to God in desperation and He soon calmed me, reassuring me that there wouldn't be a problem with my trip to Utah. The next morning early, we loaded up both my car and Deb's pickup truck so tightly we had sitting room only, filled up both vehicles, and started out on our memorable journey. The trip cost more than I had expected but the Lord provided for every need, even a motel room for the night so we could get some much needed rest on the way out.

After two long days of driving we finally arrived at Wanda's home. "Your Utah nursing license arrived today, too!" Wanda exclaimed. I could tell that she was pleasantly surprised about this "right on time" arrival. Thanks to the Lord's favor and intervention, I got to start my new job in a couple of days after I arrived. I stayed with Wanda and Walt until I got my first paycheck.

Then, I moved into a beautiful furnished basement apartment of my own in the country near Riverton where Wanda and Walt lived. The Lord even provided me with a garage of my own to park my new car in. The mountains were breathtakingly beautiful and I felt very close to God here in my new place. When the first snowfall arrived I got so excited, I felt like a child again. I rejoiced and danced before the Lord in worship. I hadn't been happy to see snow for many years. I sat soaking in the hot tub in the shelter on the back patio, watching the snow blanket the ground from the window. The mountain air was intoxicating to me, not to mention very exhilarating, and I enjoyed it immensely.

As I went joyfully and peacefully about my duties at the hospital, I felt many eyes watching me intently. Several of the Mormon ladies were intrigued with my reactions to the sometimes "not too pleasant circumstances" that confronted me. Finally, curiosity got the best of one of them so she asked me, "What makes you so different from everyone else?"

I smiled and said, "It's because Jesus lives in my heart!" Of course, that opened the door for more conversation and testimonies of how Jesus had changed my life. Several of the staff members also asked me how I could have so much peace and joy all the time. The Lord allowed me to plant seeds of faith everywhere I went. This was an awesome opportunity to share the gospel of Jesus Christ with them.

A few weeks after moving to Utah, I was checking my e-mails one evening, when an old friend sent me an instant message. My daughter had introduced me to John online about five years before this, and after hearing about his situation, I had started praying for him and his wife who had cancer. He was trying to care for her so this gave me an opportunity to be used by the Lord in prayer and ministry. We had talked online from time to time but I hadn't heard anything from him for over six months, so I was surprised. "Where are you now?" he inquired.

"I am living in Utah near Salt Lake City," I responded. The last time we had talked he was still in California.

"My wife died a few months ago and I couldn't stand to stay in California. I am living in Logan, Utah about seventy miles from Salt Lake City," he said. Somehow, I felt that this was more than just coincidence, both of us moving to Utah around the same time, especially from two different directions when we hadn't even talked for a long time. As we chatted we made plans to meet the following Sunday after church to go out for dinner.

John met me on the parking lot of my church after the service Sunday and we each took our own cars to Denny's. We felt an instant connection and enjoyed getting to know one another better. He invited me to come meet his daughter and family the next weekend in Logan.

We all went out to dinner together and she and her family immediately welcomed me into the family. Everything was moving along pretty well for me in my new place and new relationships.

However, my faith was shaken one night in February of 2002, when my daughter sent me an instant message on the Internet where we were chatting. "Uncle John and Jean (his fiancé) were found dead in a field in Missouri. Apparently they committed a double suicide from the way it seems," she sadly told me.

My brother John had been saved and gave his life to Jesus when he was in prison, was baptized in the Holy Spirit, and loved the Lord with all his heart. I found it very difficult to believe what I was reading and immediately started crying out to the Lord as fear gripped my heart that he might have gone to eternal torment. I had always heard that when people committed suicide, they lost their salvation and went to hell. Immediately, the Holy Spirit spoke to my heart. "That is a manmade doctrine and not of God! John and Jean are both in heaven with Jesus at this very moment!" He said.

Immediately after that the Lord gave me a poem about my brother and his fiancé that brought me peace. I was so thankful. I shared this message of hope with Sandy to help her receive the comfort of God since she was so close to her uncle John.

"I don't know how it will happen but somehow the Lord will make a way for me to come home to be with you and my family," I messaged her.

"John, I have bad news from Illinois. My brother and his fiancé were found dead in Missouri just a little while ago. Please pray that the Lord will make a way for me to get back to Illinois to be with my family," I told him when I called him.

Without hesitation he replied, "I will drive you back to Illinois."

Since I didn't have any money to fly I accepted his offer. I made the phone calls I needed to make, including one to my daughter to let her know that John was bringing me home, and I packed my clothes for the trip. After a couple of hours John came to pick me up and we were on our way. Once again God had proven His faithfulness to me to provide for my every need, and He brought me comfort and peace in the midst of tragedy.

Our trip to Illinois gave us many opportunities to get to know each other better and to talk openly and freely. I knew that God was working in both of our lives mightily.

When we arrived at my daughter's home her father was there too. "John, this is Sandy's father Don," I said as I introduced him.

"You had better be watching her closely because she can be very mean," Don remarked.

John immediately smiled back at him and replied, "I got the best part of her. She isn't the same now since she knows the Lord."

That put a hush on that kidding conversation. They got along very well and John was welcomed into our family. Everyone including Don (my ex-husband) could see that we were a great fit together, and they were thankful that he had brought me back home.

John stood at my side during my brother's graveside services in the midst of a winter storm and I found great comfort in his support. After the services we proceeded to my brother Frank's home to eat a good meal and fellowship before we started our long journey back to Utah.

The longer we drove together, the deeper I fell in love with John, and the more I could see the hand of the Lord at work within him. Father God impressed upon me, "Take it slow and easy with him because he isn't ready to hear much about your relationship with Jesus. He won't understand it yet."

A few weeks before this trip, I had sustained a back injury while on my job. I now suffered with a lot of pain in my low back, radiating down my right leg. After a consultation with my doctor I was referred to an orthopedic surgeon in Salt Lake City, who started giving me injections in my back and hip joint. John was faithful to take me to my doctors' appointments and he waited patiently for me to finish each one. After several treatments and physical therapy, my doctor placed me on a fifty pound lifting restriction with no stooping, pushing, pulling, or overhead lifting. On my way home that day, I took my slip from the doctor with the lifting restriction to the human resources office at work and I was immediately terminated from my job.

The Lord had already prepared me for this blow but it was still hard to take, although I knew it was all a part of His plan. As I drove home that day I prayed, "God, I know somehow You will take care of me in my time of need just as You have always done. Please help me to trust You completely and not to speak any doubt or fear in Jesus' name."

Because John hadn't gone with me to the doctor this time, I called him after I got home to let him know what had happened. "John, I have some bad news. Because my doctor placed me on a lifting restriction, HealthSouth fired me from my job."

"What are you going to do now?" he asked.

"I'm just going to pray and trust the Lord to take care of me because I know He will," was my reply. There was a moment of silence on the other end of the phone and it wasn't very long until our conversation ended. My rent was five-hundred fifty dollars per month, and since my insurance was gone with my job, I had to completely depend on God for everything.

That evening John called me. "Eric and Tessa have invited you to stay with them in their spare bedroom until you get back on your feet and it won't cost you a thing," he said. I knew in my heart that this was the provision God had given me for this season in my life so I readily accepted that invitation.

I explained the situation to my landlady, who was sad for me and hated to lose me as a tenant. John and Eric made plans to move my things the following weekend to Logan where Tessa and Eric lived.

CHAPTER 11
MY NEW LIFESTYLE

I quickly grew to love Tessa, Eric, and their red-haired daughter Haley. They loved me too. They didn't mind giving me the space and the time alone with the Lord that I was used to having. My life became a witness to them for Jesus Christ because I kept Him first in everything. God was changing each of us a little bit every day as we learned more about one another. They believed in the Mormon faith however. So I started praying and searching for a church close by that believed the way I did. I found an Assembly of God church and discovered a warm, loving church family there who readily accepted and welcomed me into their fellowship.

"Barbara, will you marry me?" John asked me one day in March. I could see the hand of God tugging at his heart and the Holy Spirit drawing him closer each day. I believed with all my heart that God would pull him out of the Mormon Church and set him free to live the life Jesus died to give him.

"Yes, I will," I answered with a big smile. I accepted without any hesitation because I felt in my heart and spirit that this was the beginning of the new life God had promised me.

I had never had a formal wedding before, but since this was my desire, John paid for the wedding as a gift to me. Because of the distance, none of my family could make it to the wedding, but we had a lot of guests from John's church and were married by his bishop in a beautiful ceremony. The anointing was so strong that day that I could barely walk up the aisle to meet my groom. On my way I heard the Lord whisper to me, "You are one of the most beautiful brides I have ever seen!"

Tessa and Eric blessed us with our first night together at a bed and breakfast in Logan as our wedding gift and we really enjoyed it. The next day we left on our honeymoon, which was yet another new and exciting experience for me. John took me to California to Disneyland, Universal Studios, and to meet more of his family who still lived there. We stayed in fine motels and ate like royalty, a real treat for a farm girl from the Midwest. We felt like kids again and we got a lot of strange looks when we told people we were on our honeymoon. John's nephew taught me how to kayak in the ocean, a real leap of faith, considering I didn't even know how to swim, but I thoroughly enjoyed it.

After our honeymoon we settled into John's home in Logan, so he opened a joint checking account for the household expenses and put me in charge of it. He told me, "If you are in the store someplace and you see something you want just go ahead and get it."

He was surprised when I told him, "I have no idea how to do that because it is something I haven't ever had enough money to do before." Each month he deposited more than enough for the household expenses so I started to buy something once in a while just because I wanted it. I truly enjoyed staying home, cleaning, cooking, and doing special things for my husband, which was a drastic change for me.

We prayed together, studied the scriptures, and spent time talking about the Lord each day. Soon the Lord impressed upon my heart, "I want you to go to church with John in the afternoons after you get home from your church, to learn more about his faith." When I told

John, he was surprised at this decision, but he seemed happy to have me by his side in the sacrament meetings at his church.

I had felt prompted to sign a prenuptial agreement with John, to prove to him that I wasn't marrying him for his money but because I loved him. I started working at a nursing home in Logan to pay my own prior obligations, including my car payment. However, I found it was impossible to continue very long due to the pain in my back and hip. I was very thankful that John never made a big deal out of my quitting work.

After three months of a wonderfully blessed marriage relationship, I started sensing a tension between us that wasn't there before. I believed John was struggling with some issues but he wouldn't discuss them with me. One day when he came home from his "mission" he said, "I have a meeting with the bishop tonight and I would like for you to come with me." "Sure, honey, that won't be a problem for me," I responded nervously.

"Next Sunday afternoon I will be installing John as a High Priest in the church," the bishop announced to me after we sat down in his office.

"What does that mean?" I asked hesitantly.

The bishop explained to me, "To obtain this high calling John had to prove himself worthy and he has done that in the eyes of the church."

The rest of that meeting is lost in space somewhere for me because my heart sank. I knew that meant he belonged to the church instead of God from that point on. I did attend the ceremony with him as a loyal wife should, even though my heart was breaking. From that moment on our marriage quickly fell apart.

The next two weeks were pure hell on earth because John seemed to shut me out of his life. He worked Monday through Friday on his "mission" for his church. When he came home each evening, instead of the usual kiss and "How are you?" greeting, he went straight to our bedroom, closed the door, and went to bed.

"John, what is wrong? Is there anything I can do for you?" I frequently asked.

"No, just leave me alone," he replied coldly. That always ended any conversation I had hoped to have with him. There was hardly ever any kind of communication between us during this time.

I had to pray now for an abundance of God's grace to help me so I would not spoil my witness for the Lord. I felt totally devastated and abandoned by my new husband.

"How could this happen, Lord?" was my plea. "Is this the way a 'High Priest' is supposed to treat his wife?" I asked with tears streaming down my face. "I don't understand how quickly everything can change in such a wonderful loving relationship!" As I sought the Lord in my desperation, He brought me comfort, the peace that surpassed all understanding and the confidence of knowing that God was still in control of my life and my destiny. God's grace and the anointing were so strong that I managed to keep walking in the Spirit instead of my flesh. I wanted so badly to demand explanation and attention from John. I couldn't stay angry with him, no matter how much I wanted to, and I couldn't open my mouth with inappropriate words because I had asked the Lord to help me not to speak anything I would regret. This was an extreme test of my faith and my determination to live a life pleasing to God.

Finally, the dreaded morning came when it all surfaced and things broke loose. John awakened that Sunday morning laying in a pool of sweat, shaking all over with fear written all over his face.

Trembling, he asked me, "Tell me, Barb, is this the way it is going to be when I go to hell?"

I looked at him in shock but I knew immediately that he had a bac dream. As he told me about the dream, I couldn't answer his question. "All I can tell you, John, is that the dream was for a purpose. You will have to talk to God about it." I knew that God had opened his eyes to the truth in the Spirit. I got ready for church and kissed him goodbye when I left, telling him I would see him later.

Usually John was gone to his own church by the time I got home, but today he was lying in bed awake struggling with what to say. "Are you sick?" I asked.

"No, I have been thinking about us. Barb, our marriage was a big mistake. You will have to leave here because you are just too much of a 'Jesus freak'! I just can't deal with that anymore!" he answered.

My heart was shattered. I responded, "God doesn't make mistakes and I know that God put us together." I never raised my voice or got angry with him. "Thank you for the compliment of 'Jesus freak'," I added. "I have been called a lot worse things in my life!"

After that, I left the room and went outside to find a place to be alone with the Lord and to ponder what I had just heard. I cried out to the Lord, "Now what, God? Where do I go and what do I do?"

In my heart, in that still, small, sweet voice of Jesus, I heard Him reply, "Go peacefully and quietly back toward Oklahoma to a place I will show you when you get there. Don't hold any bitterness or anger toward John for what has happened but keep praying for him!"

After I calmed down and got my composure back, I slowly walked back into our bedroom. "John, I will leave quietly and peacefully because you have asked me to," I told him with a few tears running down my cheeks. Then I called my family to let them know I was moving back to Oklahoma and what had happened. I started sorting, packing up my things, and preparing for the long journey ahead of me. I gave away a lot of my belongings to make room in my car for the essentials because I couldn't afford a U-Haul trailer. I took very little of what we had been given to us as wedding gifts.

"You can store what you want to keep for another trip in my garage if you want to because you will have to come back for court anyway," John said. So I carefully sorted what I couldn't pack into my car and piled it all together in one corner of the garage out of his way.

On Monday morning John approached me as if nothing had happened between us. "Barb, will you go with me to choose some roses for the front yard for landscaping?" he asked.

I never quite understood this but I went willingly and enjoyed our time together. He took me out to lunch and we had a great day of conversation and fellowship. Upon our return to the house, I started loading up my car for departure on Tuesday, packing it so tightly that I only had room enough to sit up straight to drive.

On Tuesday morning as I was getting ready to pull out of the drive, John handed me $500 in cash. "This will help you make your trip back to Oklahoma. I want to be sure you have enough to get a motel room and a hot meal. You should have enough left over to get a place of your own whenever you arrive wherever you are going," he said. "I wish you all the best, Barb."

"I might be gone from your sight, John, but just because I am not with you physically doesn't mean I won't be near you spiritually. I will be lifting you up to God daily in prayer that He will open your eyes to the truth of Jesus Christ our Lord, until I am assured that you have either surrendered your life to Him or the Lord impresses upon me to stop praying for you," I said with a smile as I drove away.

CHAPTER 12
FINDING MY WAY BY FAITH

My first stop on my long journey back to Oklahoma was an appointment with an orthopedic doctor in Salt Lake City, which had been set up by HealthSouth's attorney for my workman's compensation case against them.

As I left Salt Lake City, I had a supernatural peace and confidence in the Lord, knowing that He would take very good care of me. He had never left me nor forsaken me, just as the Bible says in Deuteronomy 31:8. I knew in my heart that He had already gone before me to prepare everything along the way. As I cruised along the Interstate, I opened up to God and poured out my emotions over my shattered heart and dreams. "God, what happened to that awesome marriage that You gave me? Did I do something wrong?" I asked with tears streaming down my face.

"John chose his religion over a personal relationship with Me. He just couldn't understand your deep, intimate, personal relationship with Me. Neither did he want to be excommunicated from his church, which he would have been, had you stayed with him after his installation as a high priest in his organization. I give everyone his free choice and John made his, which unfortunately hurt you in the process! It wasn't your fault, My child, so don't blame yourself," I heard Him say softly in the Spirit.

I drove to Denver, Colorado before I finally decided to pull over to get a motel room for the night and a hot meal. I found a cute little "Mom and Pop" motel with a family restaurant. "Thank You so much Father, for Your abundant provisions for my life. Thank You so much for the wonderfully blessed season I have just enjoyed with John, even though it was very short," I told the Lord as I got out of the car.

As I rested and prayed for further direction in that little motel room, God impressed upon me to go to Tulsa, Oklahoma. I called my friend Deb to let her know I was on my way back to Tulsa after explaining the situation to her. "Deb, will it be all right to spend my first night back in Oklahoma at your place? I really don't have any idea of where I am going from there or how long I will be there."

"That will be great, Barb! We have so much catching up to do!" she replied.

After two long days of driving, I finally arrived at Deb's. "It's so great to see you again, Deb!" "Girl, I have missed you so much!" she replied. "I have plans for this weekend to go to Victory Christian Center here in Tulsa. They are having an Encounter Weekend with God! Will you come and go with me?"

"I would love to!" That was just what I felt that I needed. God's timing was perfect, as always, and this encounter weekend was just what "Dr. Jesus" had ordered. The weekend was truly amazing and it really helped me to see this situation differently than the enemy wanted me to believe. John had led me to believe this was a temporary separation but by Saturday I received divorce papers from his attorney at Deb's address.

On Monday, the Lord impressed upon my heart, "I want you to go visit Mike and Karen now for a few days." They were my missionary friends in Missouri so I called them.

"Sure, Barb, come on up and stay as long as you want to. We are looking forward to seeing you again," Karen answered excitedly.

I kept praying for direction for my life but all I heard the Lord say was, "Trust Me, My child, and have faith in Me!"

The Lord wouldn't allow me to take in more than just my overnight needs any place I stayed. My car was still packed with all of my belongings that I could get in it, including the computer that I used for ministering to others and for writing for the Lord. It was July and very hot so I kept praying for the Lord to protect everything in it. For the first time in my life I felt homeless and helpless, and totally out of control of my life. It was a very humbling experience, to say the least, but I gained a heart for the homeless and the lost as I sought the Lord's will for my life. I started searching for a job and a home in Missouri, thinking perhaps that was where I was supposed to settle, but every door slammed shut quickly. My prayers were partially answered when the Lord spoke to my heart, "I want you to return to Tulsa now to volunteer at Victory Christian Center as a greeter for their upcoming Word Explosion next week."

"Thank you, Mike and Karen, for your hospitality, your prayers, your fellowship and everything else. God has spoken to my heart to return to Tulsa to volunteer at Victory Christian Center next week for their Word Explosion," I explained as we sat at the breakfast table together. They told me that anytime I wanted to come back I was more than welcome, and they prayed with me for God's perfect will before I left their home.

Right before leaving I called Deb to let her know I was coming back to her place that evening.

She didn't have much to say during this phone call for some reason. The battle in my mind was horrendous as the enemy condemned me for failing at yet another marriage, especially one that God had put together. He kept taunting me with these thoughts: *"What are you going to do?" "Where are you going to go now?" "You have really messed up your life now".* I quickly took authority over Satan and his lies and cast those thoughts down. I remembered in Revelation 12 that he is called "the accuser of the brethren."

Another battle surfaced when I arrived at Deb's and received an icy and angry reception from her. "You can't stay here anymore, Barb!" she exclaimed without any explanation.

"Everything will be all right, Deb, because I have enough money left to get a motel room," I said broken hearted. "I know that tomorrow God will provide me a place to live. I love you, girl!" I said as I got back into my car to leave as I choked back the tears.

I went to a convenience store to purchase the local newspapers to start searching for a home and drove to Motel 6 to get a room for the night. Before I started combing the rental ads, I enjoyed a good hot meal to prepare me for a long night of prayer.

When I got back to my room I called my daughter. "Sandy, I am in Tulsa, Oklahoma now. This is where the Lord wants me to be for a while so I am going to find a place to rent tonight and I will let you know my new address as soon as I get one. Don't worry about me because the Lord will provide for my every need," I reassured her.

After hanging up I started diligently praying, searching the papers and circling the ads of the rental places that I thought I could afford. I called the ones that listed phone numbers in the ads. It was very disheartening as the doors slammed shut in my face, one right after another. Once more the enemy came in like a flood with those negative thoughts. I cried and prayed until three in the morning when I finally went to sleep.

I got back up at six, took my shower, and went to a restaurant to enjoy a good hot breakfast and coffee. When I got back to the motel room, I got desperately serious with God in my search for a home. The only phone number where I received an answer was for some rental trailers in Kiefer, Oklahoma. "How soon may I come to look at them?" I inquired.

"How soon can you be here?" the landlady asked. I told her I would come on now if she could meet me there and I asked for directions.

It was very unsettling for me as I looked at several trailers in this rundown little trailer park, because they were all very dirty and needed a lot of repairs. I felt demoted and couldn't understand God's plan at all, but I knew that I had to make a decision quickly because I was running out of money. "I have very limited funds right now because I just got back from Utah a few days ago. I don't have the money for the deposit, just the rent." I reluctantly told her.

"I tell you what I will do. If you will clean the one you choose yourself, I will waive the deposit for you. I know it will take a lot of time and work," she replied. I settled on the one that needed the least work and I paid the rent.

"Is there someone who could move the mattress and box springs from the first trailer I saw to this one so I can have something to sleep on?" I inquired.

"I will have my maintenance man to move them here for you and I will have him to fix your air conditioner this afternoon," she replied.

Whoever had lived in this trailer before had left a sofa and a broken chest of drawers. "God, please give me the strength and energy I need to clean up this mess and make it decent," I prayed. I spent the afternoon picking up trash and messes. I made a list of what I needed to start cleaning and repairing. After the maintenance man left, I drove to the local Wal-Mart Supercenter to get the things I needed including bed linens, towels, washcloths, cleaning supplies of all kinds, hammer, and nails, etc.

God gave me creative ideas about how to fix the place up and after a few days I had it shining clean and looking like a home should. I praised Him and thanked Him for our new home, and dedicated it to His service after anointing it. He showed me that He had allowed me to go through this season to give me a heart for the homeless, and so that I wouldn't be so quick to judge others by their appearance and the conditions they live in. I had now experienced what it felt like to not have a home of my own, to not know where I would lay my head at night, or where I would get my next meal.

"Thank You so much, Father God, for all my friends and family, and that I have never had to sleep under a bridge like so many do. Please keep me humble because I just don't know what others have been through to bring them to their place of desperation." He taught me the true meaning of humility and stripped me of my pride, which I didn't realize I had.

"Hey, Deb, I found a place to live in Kiefer and I finally got it fit for company. Why don't you come visit me soon?" I asked Deb whenever I called her. She came down that following weekend and took me to several yard sales to find the other things I still needed. We found God's favor everywhere we went that day. Whenever people found out that I was starting over and didn't have much money, they opened up their hearts and blessed me with many different things, including a bed frame which I really needed. We came back to my trailer that day with a pickup load of needed household items for almost no money at all. One of my neighbors had brought by a kitchen table and chairs and left them on my front porch while we were gone. Deb's boss had given her a microwave, which she brought down with her and gave it to me. My humble little abode had suddenly become fully furnished and was even kind of cute, making it "home sweet home" to me and the Lord.

Whenever I attended the meeting for the volunteers at Victory

Christian Center for Word Explosion, I was readily and cheerfully accepted as one of the greeters. I volunteered for both the daytime and evening services, so I heard nearly all of the speakers and teachings that week. My heart was overflowing with God's Word by the end of that week. I knew in my heart that Jesus had healed a lot of the wounds I had sustained in my last venture with John. God is so awesome! I started attending church regularly at Victory Christian Center every time the doors were open. Although it was a huge church, I quickly built relationships with the people near where I sat each week. This started another cycle of growth in my spiritual walk with the Lord.

When I started receiving unemployment benefits, my checks were too small to cover all the bills I had to pay. I checked with the State Board of Nursing about having my Oklahoma nursing license reinstated but because it was going to cost $125, I couldn't proceed right away. I started searching for other jobs that I could do but was very limited because I had almost always been a nurse. I worked a couple of days at a small doctor's office as a receptionist but they terminated me quickly because I was too slow for the position. Victory's food pantry became a tremendous blessing to me because they provided food for my table.

In desperation I cried out to God, "Lord, I just don't know what I am supposed to do about my dilemma! I have tried all the angles that I know. Will You please help me to understand Your guidance and direction?"

Soon, the answer came to me, "Call the Department of Rehabilitation Services to ask if they will retrain you for another career." Because of my back problems, they quickly approved me and paid for classes at the local community college for medical office management.

By the end of November, Victory Christian Center had outgrown their building. After a lot of prayer, they decided to build a new building and campus. They were holding home meetings to share with small groups from the congregation their plans for the new project and to ask for pledges so that they could pay cash for the construction. Although I didn't have much income, I felt led to make a small pledge and started praying about which meeting to attend.

The day before the last meetings the answer came very specifically. I called Eunice, the hostess of one of them, to see if she still had room for one more person and she joyfully said, "Yes". The directions she gave me to her home were very clear, but for some reason, I kept missing my turns and got detoured. I was a little bit late. I apologized but I didn't feel so bad when a minister from Victory came in and shared the same type of story about his experience driving to this meeting.

"I thought about just going back home but the Holy Spirit kept prompting me to press on and come anyway." We all knew this was a divine appointment God had arranged and that the enemy had tried to stop it from happening. After watching the presentation and fellowship, Eunice asked me where I worked. I explained my situation and that I wasn't working anywhere right now. I hadn't told anyone that this next unemployment check was the last one, and after that one, I would have no income at all. The minister who was late suggested we all pray for my situation, so he slipped his arm around me to pray. I felt as if the Lord's wings of love were wrapped around me and warmth overtook me as we started to pray.

"Barbara, I sense that the Lord is telling me to open my home to you. I have a spare room you can stay in until you can get back on your feet," Eunice said.

"I will pray about it and let you know," I responded.

"I sense in my spirit that your last unemployment check will be delivered next week. Is this true?" she continued.

"I'm afraid it is," I replied hesitantly.

The pastor slipped a twenty dollar bill into my hand after that. "The

Lord told me you need it," he added. I was so thankful for my newly found family and friends and for God's provisions for me.

Tears streamed from my eyes as I thanked them all.

After a few short prayers about the situation, the Lord showed me that I was to accept Eunice's offer to move into her home. I called her to let her know and to make arrangements. Because I had accumulated a whole house full of decent furniture and household goods with no place to store them, I began praying about what to do with everything. The Lord impressed me to call the minister at the Victory Dream Center and donate it if someone could come haul it all away.

On moving day the pastor and some helpers came to pick up the household furnishings. "Thank you so much for this blessing! It is just in time because we have someone whose home burned last night and she lost everything!" he said. What a wonderful thing to be able to bless someone else with the blessings I had received!

After they left, I moved what I had left to Eunice's home. I stored a lot of it in her garage because I didn't need it in my room. "Eunice, I really appreciate this huge blessing so that I can get back on my feet again. Thank you so much for being obedient to the Holy Spirit!"

This blessing allowed me to use my last unemployment check to get my nursing license reinstated in Oklahoma. Just as soon as I got my nursing license back, I started praying about work and searching for a job. Soon after that I received a position with a temporary agency and started working part-time at the David L. Moss Correctional Center in Tulsa as a second job. Finally, I had some decent income, so I paid Eunice a little out of each paycheck for my room and board. It took a while to catch up on all my payments again but little by little, with the help of the Lord, I got everything paid up.

After Christmas I moved into an efficiency apartment in Sapulpa, closer to my school and to Deb. There were several rental units in the apartment building, so this gave me a lot of opportunities to share the love of Jesus with others and be a witness for Him.

"Mom, Christa and I have found a wonderful little home for us that we can buy near the lake outside of Checotah!" my oldest son Nick said whenever he called me. "Can you come down to see it and meet our new landlord? It is completely furnished." I was really excited for them since this would be their first home of their own.

"Sure, son, I would love to," I replied. I had prayed for favor for them to be able to get the right home and it was amazing how it all worked out. It was so beautifully furnished and I really liked that quiet, peaceful, lake community.

"Doc, do you have any more mobile homes for sale here?" I asked his new landlord.

"Not now, but when we get another one, I will call you," he responded.

A couple of months later, Doc called me and made arrangements for me to see a newer mobile home that he had just acquired. It was beautiful and I wanted it but the payments were too high for me at that time. "I will keep you in mind if I get any more homes available," he told me after we had discussed the deal.

In April Doc called again, "Barbara, I have another mobile home we have just purchased. We are clearing the land for it now. Would you like to come check it out this weekend?"

"I sure would! Thank you so much for not giving up on me," I replied.

His wife Bina was there cleaning the inside when I got there to see it. "I wanted to have it all done before you saw it," she said, "but I didn't quite get it finished." I knew the moment I walked in it was the one God had chosen for me. It was beautiful and fit my taste perfectly with the design, colors, and layout I desired. It had two bedrooms and two full baths. I was very excited about it and anxious to move in.

Where I worked in Tulsa was at least seventy miles one way from my new home, so I started looking for a job closer to Checotah. I quickly obtained a position at the cardiology clinic in Muskogee, twenty miles away from my new home. After working out my notice of resignation at the correctional center, I drove back and forth from Sapulpa. I anxiously waited for Doc and Bina to get my mobile home ready for me to move into. It took two to three weeks to get it finished and everything hooked up.

Finally, after what seemed to me to be an eternity, on April 26, 2003, I moved into my new home the Lord had blessed me with. After signing the contracts, Bina, Doc, Nick, Christa, and my granddaughter Heather, and I went to see my new home. As I walked in the front door, tears started flowing down my cheeks like a river and Bina joined me with some of her own tears. Doc asked, "Don't you like it?"

"I love it and am very happy with it. These are tears of joy!" I replied.

After everyone left that day, I started crying and fell to my knees in worship and praise to the Lord. I was in awe of God's love and the gifts He had given me, especially since I never thought I would have anything so beautiful again. Bina had fully furnished this home for me with exactly what I had asked for and there were flower arrangements everywhere! She had even hung a very large picture of a mountain scene on one of my living room walls. I knew without a shadow of a doubt that the Lord Himself had helped her to decorate it uniquely for me. As I spent time basking in His presence, memories of the lies Satan had told me on my way back from Utah flooded my mind.

Then I heard the Lord's still small voice, "What do you think now?"

"Satan is a liar! Father God, it is so much more beautiful and wonderful than I had ever imagined! I love You so much! Thank You, thank You, thank You for your faithfulness to me, for replacing what the enemy has stolen from me, and giving me even better than I had before!" I knew in my heart this was my reward for being obedient, standing on God's Word, and believing in Him. I dedicated this home to His service and anointed it with oil. This was our home (the Lord's and mine) and if I ever left, it would be because the Lord told me to leave, not because someone else told me I had to leave.

"Father, where would You like for me to attend church now?" I inquired of the Lord. I felt the Holy Spirit leading me to check out a church that one of the worship leaders in the Victory Singles group had told me about. She knew the couple who ministered at New Life Christian Center in Stigler, Oklahoma. I looked up directions to the church on the Internet and printed them out for the next Sunday. I knew that God was taking me a whole new direction in my life and I was very excited about my new home and a new church family too. When I called the church, the answering machine announced the service times.

I left home the next Sunday in what I thought was plenty of time to get there. Unfortunately, I took a wrong turn and got lost on my way, so I arrived just as the service was dismissing. "I'm sorry I am so late," I told the senior pastor. "I took a wrong turn and got lost on my way here. May I give you my tithe for this week?" I asked.

"Sure, if you want to," Pastor Rick replied, surprised and amazed. "My wife, Pastor Angela, is out of the country ministering but she will be back next week. I'm quite sure she would love to meet you!"

I laughed as I inquired, "So what time do your services start here? I will be on time next week since I now know how to get here." Even though it was forty-two miles one way to church, I knew this was where the Lord was planting me for this new season. I was very comfortable with the people and I felt the love of God abundantly, even as I entered the front foyer.

I continued working at the clinic in Muskogee until I got a job even closer to my new home. I made more money in the nursing home at Eufaula, Oklahoma. My daughter-in-law Christa was a nurse's aide so she started working with me at the nursing home. It didn't take me long to realize that I was burned out on nursing home work and needed something different. At the nursing home, I met Edith, a part-time nurse, who also worked full time for a home health agency. Her granddaughter was very ill and needed prayer. This opened up an opportunity I wasn't expecting. I prayed with her for her granddaughter and built a good relationship with her. As we were talking one day about her other job, the Lord dropped in my spirit to ask her if they needed any more L,P,N.'s.

"As a matter of fact, they do need another one for a case manager position. Have you ever had any experience in this area?"

"No, I haven't," I replied. "What does a case manager do?"

As she explained what the position involved, it sounded like the ideal job so I asked her to bring me an application.

After I had completed the application and turned it in, it took several phone calls before I was honored with an interview with the administrator. The very minute I arrived in the office I felt the presence of the Lord. The two receptionists, Phyllis and Debbie were very wonderful, warm, friendly ladies. When Christie the administrator called me in for my interview, I felt an immediate click with her and discovered she too was a Christian. She noted in my job history how much I had moved around from place to place.

"So if I hire you for this position, how long will you stay with me? It requires you to have more training you know, which I will have to pay for," she said looking me in the eyes.

"I can't promise you anything except that I will stay until the Lord tells me to move on," I answered boldly.

She looked at me and smiled and said, "Good answer!" She immediately awarded me the position, so that day I gave my two weeks' notice of resignation at the nursing home.

CHAPTER 13
ENJOYING MY GREAT NEW LIFE

I had never had an office position where I had my own desk and computer but I felt like God had promoted me. Even though I took a slight cut in pay, my schedule was straight days with weekends off, paid holidays, and vacation after six months. As we got to know each other, all of us in the office became one big happy Christian family. Sandy, the other new case manager, and I attended the required classes together in Tulsa. This position was something totally different from anything I had ever done before. I was in charge of meeting my consumers' needs, and I scheduled my own home visits. I arranged meetings with them and their families to determine what they needed to allow them to stay in their own homes instead of having to go to a nursing home. Nurse visits with weekly medication setups were included for some consumers, as well as monthly case management meetings in the homes for all of them. My position included making a lot of telephone calls and problem solving when things didn't go right. I thoroughly enjoyed every bit of my new assignment. Documentation and creating care plans was a big portion of my job and required the use of a computer for long hours.

Within two months I got my first raise. One afternoon just about closing time, Christie approached me. "Barb, I have something for you and I won't take no for an answer. The Lord shared with me that you don't have any meat in your home, so I want to bless you with some from our freezer," she said. "Would it offend you if Rick and I bought you some groceries and brought them to you this evening?"

"No, it wouldn't offend me at all," I said with tears welling up in my eyes. I hadn't mentioned the struggle I was having making ends meet but God knew my needs and they were the vessels He had chosen to meet those needs. "Thank you so much and may God bless you guys!" They arrived at my house around 7:30 that evening and filled my cabinets and refrigerator with everything that I would enjoy. What a blessing!

"Barb, I would like to take you with us and our church group when we go to do a free sale," Christie said. "It is a mission trip to southern Texas and we will go over into Mexico to do some shopping while we are there."

"Sure! I would love to go with you!" I responded with tears welling up in my eyes. I was truly thrilled and honored to be invited on my very first mission trip. How could I possibly say no when the desire for missions was so deeply implanted in my heart?

While we were in Mexico, Christie bought me a genuine Mexican dress and a tambourine to play at church, another new thing the Lord gave me a desire to do. God was opening doors for me like I had never seen before and was blessing me more than I could have imagined. I truly looked forward to going to work each day.

One morning in my prayer time the Lord asked me, "How do you like your new full time job and ministry all rolled into one?"

"I hadn't really thought about it that way before but that is just what it is," I responded. I often got to pray with my consumers and they looked forward to my visits because of the presence of the Lord in my life. "Thank You so very much, Lord! This position is truly a gift from You! I love You so much!"

As I continued attending New Life Christian Center in Stigler, I was rapidly promoted there by the Lord also. Pastor Angela and I clicked immediately and our relationship became very special. I became part of the intercessory prayer team, a greeter at the door of the church before services, and an armor bearer for Pastor Angela. As I sat under the anointed teaching of Pastors Rick and Angela, I grew in faith and in my walk with God by leaps and bounds. Because the Holy Spirit was allowed to move freely there, we had frequent visitations from the Lord, healing, and deliverance of people from the enemy's chains of bondage. It was here that I learned about fasting and first fruits offerings and the benefits from being obedient to the Lord. Every time I came up short of cash, the Lord impressed someone to give me ten or twenty dollars to help me out. I was amazed at the way these people gave to one another in times of need, as they were being led by the Lord. My daughter-in-law Christa and my granddaughter Heather started going to church with me and they were both growing closer to the Lord and being blessed too. God was answering my prayers quickly and abundantly. I know now that I was enjoying true "Kingdom Prosperity" with peace, hope, joy, provisions, a beautiful home and life, and wonderful family and friends. My personal relationship with Jesus Christ was worth more than anything in the whole world to me.

I enjoyed the peace and tranquility of my new country home by the lake and nearly every evening after work, I walked to the lake to enjoy the sunset and praise the Lord for the beauty surrounding me. I spent a lot of time on my front porch with my coffee, especially in the early mornings, enjoying quiet time with the Lord and listening to the birds singing their praises to God. Many times I was inspired to write poetry while sitting on my front porch at the cute little table Bina had strategically placed there for me. I didn't mind doing my own yard work, although sometimes it was tough after working all week.

One Wednesday evening on my way to church, the Lord suddenly prompted me to pick up a hitch hiker right outside of Checotah. He seemed hesitant at first so I rolled down the window on the passenger side of the car. "Hi, I'm Barbara. Get in, sir!" He reluctantly climbed in the passenger seat after putting his things in the back seat.

"Are you sure about this?" he asked.

"Of course I am. The Lord wanted me to give you a lift, so I know it is safe," I replied. He told me his name was Jimmy and where he was headed. After we had talked a little while, I invited him to go to church with me and finally he consented. He and our youth pastor hit it off right away and the Lord gave him a prophetic message through that pastor. Jimmy was shocked by what he had just experienced with the Lord.

"Where do you want out?" I asked him when we got back to the Interstate after church. It was late and dark so the chances for him getting a ride were very slim. After praying in my heart about what to do I asked him, "Why don't you just come home with me to spend the night in the guest room and I will take you out to the Interstate in the morning to catch a ride?"

He reluctantly accepted and as I pulled off the Interstate on the ramp to go back to my home, he asked, "What's your husband going to say?"

"Nothing because Jesus is my husband and He was the one who asked me to bring you back to our home," I replied boldly.

He looked shocked so I then explained the rules of our home to him. "No alcohol, smoking, drugs, cursing, or anything displeasing to the Lord. It is His home and is used for His service only!" He was amazed when he entered our home and I showed him to the guest room and the guest bathroom that he would be using. It was at the opposite end of the mobile home from my bedroom. You are free to stay as long as you want so long as you help me take care of the yard and home repairs as needed. I do encourage you to find a job if you are going to stay very long so you will have your own money."

The next evening, when I got home from work, he was still there so after supper we walked to the lake. As we walked, Jimmy opened up to me about some of the issues in his life and I was surprised at how comfortable he felt telling me these things. After we got back to the house, he was tired, so he sat down and we prayed together for the Lord to deliver him. After that it was amazing to watch a wonderful blanket of peace come over him and he fell asleep in his bed.

The following Monday morning, I awakened at four o'clock as usual, but in the spirit I sensed a great battle going on so I started praying against it. I couldn't seem to get a breakthrough, so around six I knocked on Jimmy's door and asked him to come out to pray with me. After praying together in agreement, I felt peace and thanked him for getting up.

Just as I was getting ready to leave the office that morning to go see some of my consumers, I received a phone call from my son Nick. "Mom, Christa has been hit by a train!" he cried out. Christa had recently started working for this same home health agency as a provider and home health aide. She was on her way to see her last consumer of the day when the accident happened.

"Oh, my God!" I screamed out. Everyone in the office came running to see what was wrong. I immediately took authority over Satan and declared Psalm 118:17 over Christa that "She will live and not die to declare the works of the Lord in the earth!" I tearfully told them what Nick had just told me and that I had to leave immediately. Sandy said she would go see my consumers and not to worry about it.

Nick was at my house when I got there and was extremely upset crying out, "Why is God taking Christa away from me?"

"God is not taking her away, Nick, she is going to live!" I retaliated.

My heart wrenched for him that moment because I felt his pain, but he didn't know Jesus like I did, so he didn't understand. Christa had just rededicated her life to Jesus in November the year before this in our church. "Nick, what do you want to do about Heather? Christie volunteered to pick her up from school and keep her as long as she needs to." We both agreed that Heather didn't need to know about this yet, so he agreed to let me call Christie to accept her offer.

Nick said when he got the call, the ambulance personnel were getting ready to Medi-Flight Christa to Tulsa, so we headed for Tulsa. I told Jimmy I felt that he should go with us too. When we got to the emergency room at the hospital the doctors were still working on her, so we spent some time in the waiting room while her other family members were notified and arrived. Finally, the doctor came out to bring us the news.

"She has sustained a head injury, broke off some teeth, and her right ear was severed, but she has no broken bones and no internal injuries that we can find. A plastic surgeon was on duty when she arrived so he sewed her ear back on right away." he told us, "I would prefer that only the immediate family go in to see her briefly because she is under heavy sedation right now."

As Nick, Christa's dad, and I stood by her gurney, I saw her father's hand reach for Nick's and give him a reassuring squeeze. They had recently had some differences but I saw God restoring this relationship before my very eyes and was very thankful.

After we had all seen her for a few minutes, her mother Bodie asked me to go to the chapel with her to pray. We took Jimmy with us too. As we started praying for Christa, the word of the Lord came through me saying, "I Myself had her cradled in My arms when this happened!" I knew that this reassurance could only come from God and indeed He was telling us the truth. Most people who get hit by a train in a car don't live to tell about it, much less escape without any broken bones or internal injuries. Now the truth had been revealed about the spiritual battle that Jesus, Jimmy, and I had won this morning through our prayers of faith. The enemy tried to take her out but the blood of Jesus Christ we had covered her with, saved her life and gave her divine protection. Thank God I had learned to be obedient to His voice when He spoke to me to pray!

Through this tragic event the Lord also restored the relationship between Christa's mother and father which had been severed for years, and they became friends. Christa remained in the hospital in a medication induced coma until her brain stopped swelling. After she recovered some, she moved to a rehabilitation hospital for therapy.

When we went to visit her there, she told me about seeing the Lord Jesus Christ and Him talking with her while she was in the coma. The visions He had shown her while she was with Him were wonderful and gave her hope for the future. The love He had poured out to her was indescribable. She eventually recovered completely and was able to work again. The inherent power of speaking the scriptures over people's lives in faith was proven beyond a shadow of a doubt.

Jimmy stayed for about three months but backslid into his former habits, so he left voluntarily one day while I was at work. He left a note for me asking me to pray for him and said that he would be back, but I never saw him again. He had been there for the appointed season to grow in his walk with the Lord and to be my prayer partner and yard keeper. He did keep the yard beautiful for me and we enjoyed spending time together with the Lord.

Not long after that, I met a single minister from Tulsa online. After we got to know more about one another, we met in person in Tulsa. "I have written two books of poetry but have never published them," Vern said.

"That's interesting because the Lord has been ministering to me about publishing a book of the poetry He has given me with the title, 'Whispers from Heaven,'" I said. Vern liked photography and had received a new digital camera from his landlord for his birthday. As I prayed about the picture for the cover of our book, the Lord gave me a vision of a feather cloud and laid it upon my heart to share it with Vern. One Sunday he came down to eat dinner after church with me and my granddaughter Heather who was staying with me at the time.

"On my way home today, the Lord told me to pull the car over. There in the sky was the cloud you described to me, so I took a picture of it," he e-mailed me when he got home. He also e-mailed the picture to me and asked if that was something like I was looking for. Immediately, I knew the Lord had provided that particular cloud for our book cover and I was so amazed.

"It is the perfect picture! May I use it for our book?" I inquired.

"Of course, you may. That is why I took the picture," he replied. By this time I had fallen in love with Vern and was convinced that he was the godly mate God had promised me but he didn't feel the same way. He had been deeply hurt by women before and was "gun shy".

I completed our book of poetry, designed the book covers, and submitted my work to a print on demand publishing company along with the money that was required for setup. After a couple of weeks I called Vern. "Vern, I received my two proof books. Will you please proofread one of them for me?" I asked.

"Sure, I would be happy to," he replied. He took it with him to Kansas when he went to visit his dad. When he returned, I went to Tulsa to see him and to pick up my proof book. He said, "You gave me too much credit for the picture."

"Nope, I didn't," I assured him. "I was following the lead of the Holy Spirit in what I wrote in the acknowledgement section."

Shortly after that I received an e-mail from Vern ending our relationship. I was devastated and didn't understand, but as the Lord had always done, I knew in time, He would heal my broken heart again. After Whispers from Heaven was published, I sent e-mails to all on my contact list to let them know it was available, including Vern. One day when I checked the website of the publishing company to see if there were any reviews posted, there was a great review from Vern. I wrote and thanked him for writing it and for purchasing the first book online.

I received many prophecies about this book and most of them indicated that it would reach thousands of people and be a huge success. I still believe God is going to do that in His time and His way. I sold quite a few copies myself, but gave away more than I sold by the prompting of the Holy Spirit.

Sometimes I hesitated about giving them away because of the cost to both publish and purchase them, but the Lord quickly turned that attitude around. "It isn't about you," He said. "It is to help others that I have given you this precious gift."

Shortly after this book was published, God impressed upon my heart to write my autobiography. My goal was to publish it in 2006 with my income tax refund. I started writing about my life, which was very painful at times, even though I thought I had forgiven everyone and been delivered of a lot of issues. I both laughed and cried as I wrote, praised the Lord, and questioned Him about a lot of feelings I still had. It was like a giant roller coaster ride with my emotions but it was a greatly freeing experience.

In April of 2006, this book was almost finished except for the last chapter and the cover picture.

While I was in church one evening, my daughter had left a message on my cell phone for me to call her. "What's up, Sandy?" I asked.

"Daddy has had a major stroke and he isn't doing well, Momma," she replied.

"Oh, no! Do you want me to come up to be with you?" I asked, knowing the answer.

"If you can I would sure like for you to come! I am so scared!" she said. After hanging up with her, I went back into my church to pray with the pastor for guidance and direction from the Lord about when to go to Illinois.

"Father, can I wait until tomorrow so I can get some paperwork finished at work and get it in the mail?" I asked on my way home.

The answer came very quickly, "No, it cannot wait! You must go tonight as soon as you get packed!"

When I got home I called Sandy. "Hi, Sandy, it's Mom. Just as soon as I can get packed and get the car loaded, I will be on my way to Illinois. I love you very much and will see you later."

Then I made the call to Christie. "Christie, this is Barb and I have a family emergency in Illinois and must leave tonight. Will you please have Sandy M. send in my paperwork tomorrow? My daughter's father has had a major stroke and is in critical condition so I don't know when I will be back."

"Don't worry about anything, Barb. We will take good care of things here. You just go and be with your family as long as you are needed," Christie replied.

As I drove and prayed, the Lord brought back to me some powerful and beautiful memories of my marriage to Don. We were together for twenty-eight years, so we had been through a lot. Even though we hadn't served God or invited Him into our marriage, we had received many miracles and blessings through His mercy and grace. Although we had been divorced now for nine years, we were great friends. Whenever I went to back to Illinois to visit, he and I always did something special together like going out to breakfast and visiting his family.

In 2005 the Lord had spoken to me one morning in my prayer time, "I want you to bring Don to Oklahoma for a two-week visit."

"Really Lord? Are you telling me this or is it the devil?" I inquired.

"It is My voice My child. I want him to see how you live the true Christian life and allow him to sense My presence," He answered.

Our visit went extremely well considering our two totally different lifestyles. Before, he hadn't wanted anything to do with "religion" or God. On our way to Oklahoma, I explained the rules to him about the things that were allowed and not allowed and he readily accepted them. I was totally amazed that he didn't curse the whole time he was there, watched my favorite ministers on television, studied the Bible, and prayed with me. The Lord had used my life with God to plant good seeds in his heart and to draw Don to Himself. As I made my way back to Illinois this time, everything seemed very different. I knew in my heart that this might be Don's final curtain on this life.

Sandy waited at home for me to arrive before going to the hospital to see her dad, so we rode together in her vehicle. As I went into his room, I walked over to his bed, slipped my hand into his, and told him I was there. He couldn't really see because the stroke had affected his sight but he recognized my voice immediately and thanked me for being there. After all his family had left except for his niece and Sandy, I approached him to ask if he had ever given his life to Jesus.

At this cue, Sandy and Brenda left the room to leave us alone. He replied, "He doesn't want my life!"

"Yes He does!" I replied quickly. "He loves you just as much as He loves me." I backed off and went to sit down for a little while to let him think it over.

When I went back to his bedside, I asked once again, "Don, now seriously, I really do want to know if you have asked Jesus Christ into your heart to be your Lord!"

"I already have, Barbara!" He answered smiling widely. This gave me great peace because I believed he was sincere and I saw a wave of peace come over him as well.

After Sandy came back into his room, we left to go home for a while so he could rest. He was scheduled for an MRI that evening to determine the damage to his brain from the stroke, so we waited until later that evening to go back to visit. We found him heavily sedated for the MRI because he couldn't lie still. We couldn't awaken him no matter how hard we tried. So after a while we said good night and went home.

The next day, Sandy and I went to the hospital early to catch the doctor when he made his rounds, but we found Don in a coma. "The time has come for you to make some critical decisions about life support and a feeding tube," the doctor explained to Sandy. "I really don't expect him to recover," he continued. I felt her pain as her heart shattered, so I called Pastor Angela and asked her to pray with us. We laid hands on Don and one another as she prayed for him and us. We gave it all to God that day as we asked for His will to be done in Don's life.

After we prayed and I had hung up the phone, I heard the Lord say, "He has made his peace with Me and is ready to come home now." I shared this with Sandy and saw a moment of comfort come to her, but she quickly ran out of the room to do some thinking. She wasn't ready to let him go and was struggling with these very difficult decisions she was left to make as his only child and no one to help her.

As we drove back to Barry, I told her that I felt that I needed to go back to the hospital to be with him. So I drove my car back to the hospital. I took my laptop to his room with me, and as I sat at the foot of his bed watching him, I saw a supernatural peace over him that I had never seen on him before. It was as if he was resting in the arms of Jesus. As I sat there watching him, a poem started flowing from my heart like a river. I titled it "Reflections of our Years Together".

When I finished typing the poem, I walked to his bedside and sat down beside him, gently stroking his arm with tears in my eyes. "Don, please forgive me for all the pain I have caused you. Thank you so much for the many wonderful memories I have of our times together and for our beautiful daughter," I said softly, watching his eyes for any sign of a response. I felt such a strong bond and such a peace between us that I knew he had heard every word, and that he had forgiven me, even though there was no visible response.

The next morning I went to the hospital early to be with Don again and to pray for him and his family. I took my Bible with me, walked to the head of his bed, sat down, and read Psalm 23 to him, reassuring him that the Lord was his Shepherd too.

My sons had both made it back from Oklahoma by this time, and Danny came to visit first. He came to Don's bedside, kneeled in front of me, and took Don's hand. "Dad, it is Danny. I love you, Dad! Thank you for being such a great dad and for teaching me all that you have. I will never forget you," he said as tears streamed down his cheeks. My heart broke as he cried and I felt his pain, but I also felt peace between the two of them as he talked to Don.

Nick and Christa came by but Nick couldn't bring himself to come over close to the bed. He stood by the door of the room as tears welled up in his eyes. He couldn't let go, even though I encouraged him to do so.

Later on, the doctor called Sandy at home and told her, "Your dad has no brain activity that can be measured. There is nothing else we can do here for him. We will be moving him to the nursing home in Barry sometime today."

When she came to the hospital to sign papers for no life support or feeding tube, she asked us all to step out of the room to give her some time alone with her daddy. We honored her request to allow her time to tell him it was all right to go home. Afterwards, she reluctantly signed the paperwork. It was extremely difficult to watch her go through such pain because I felt helpless. But I knew that God was helping her, just as I had asked Him to do. Don was transferred to the nursing home around three that afternoon. His sister Emily came to the nursing home to be alone with him for a little while. Danny, my second granddaughter Jessica, and I went to visit him again that evening. I noticed that his vital signs were becoming unstable and his feet were cold, so I knew it wouldn't be long. The nurse called Sandy at five o'clock the next morning to tell her he had passed away, so I went to the nursing home with her to comfort and support her.

I also went with Sandy later that day to make the funeral arrangements. I was very surprised when all his family members, who were there, agreed that I should be listed in his obituary as a survivor. They all knew that in Don's eyes, I was still his wife because he had never stopped loving me. At the flower shop, the Lord led me to get a single yellow rose with a special white satin heart and a red ribbon for his casket. On the card was simply written, "Love, Barbara". It was placed at his head inside the top of the casket.

When we went to his apartment to find some needed items, I noticed pictures of the two of us sitting everywhere. We also found a letter from Don, which had been mailed to me but returned to him because the name of the city in my address was illegible. Sandy opened it and let me read it. He had written it in February. "Barb, will you please come get me? I am very sick and I need you to take care of me. I still love you very much, and will do whatever you want me to do just to be with you," it read.

I was shocked and heartbroken for a moment because I hadn't received the letter. The Lord quickly changed that thought because if

I had received it, it may have detoured me from God's plans. I probably would have gone to Illinois to rescue him. God knew what was best for both of us and He had intervened in a way we didn't understand.

I handled the visitation and the funeral pretty well until the final pass by the casket. The Lord had me to take the poem I had written in the hospital, from the picture board at the funeral home, and place it in the casket with him. As I leaned down to kiss him goodbye on his forehead, I broke into uncontrollable sobs and felt as if my heart were being ripped out. As I lost control of my emotions, so did my sons-in-law, and my daughter. I couldn't believe the way it affected me after the years we had been separated but now I knew what a real soul tie was. We proceeded to the graveside and I read "Reflections of Our Years Together" during the final services. When the graveside service was finished, I went to sit in my car to wait for the rest of the family to go to the luncheon the church was having for the family and friends. I looked up to see Jessica bringing me a single long stemmed yellow rose from one of the bouquets to take home with me in remembrance of her Grandpa. Yellow roses were always his favorites.

At the church dinner, as I was talking to Don's brother Dick and his wife Mary, I was suddenly overwhelmed with an urgency to ask their forgiveness. The Lord revealed to me that I still had bitterness and anger in my heart toward Mary for the times I had caught Don flirting with her. I started crying as I said, "Mary and Dick, I need you to forgive me for all the years that I have been bitter and angry." Neither of them acted like they knew what I was talking about until I explained it to them. "I have been holding a grudge for years because I caught Don flirting with Mary and her sister. That's why I couldn't stand to talk to you or even look you in the eyes for so long," I said feeling the sting of guilt.

They both immediately forgave me and I felt a big release as we hugged one another. Soon after we finished eating, I felt led to head back toward Oklahoma because I had to get up and go to work the next day.

As I started out on my long homeward journey, I asked the Lord, "Why did this funeral and saying goodbye to Don hit me so hard, Lord? I don't understand it."

"Now My child, you have experienced for yourself how it feels to lose someone you have been so close to for so many years. You can minister more effectively to widows and widowers since you have felt their pain," He answered. There is still an empty place in my heart where Don's love resided, but my reassurance comes from knowing that I will see him in heaven when I arrive there one day.

CHAPTER 14
UNEXPECTED CHANGES

When I got back home I wrote the last chapter of my autobiography, "Through the Valleys". It was now very clear to me that the very painful experience I had just had with becoming a "widow" was to be the final chapter. It helped me to put closure on that season of my life.

"Lord, we need a picture for the front cover on our book, now," I prayed. Soon after that, the Lord gave me a vision of the cover He wanted the book to have. It included a mountain and valley scene but I had no idea where to find a mountain in Oklahoma. As I traveled the highways, I prayed and kept looking for the ideal place but couldn't find it. I had heard about some scenery south of where I went to church that might be a possibility. So one Wednesday evening, on my way to church, I left early and took a detour. When I got close I stopped at a convenience store to ask for directions to Stigler. There was a state highway patrolman there so I asked him, "Excuse me, sir, do you know any place where I can find a mountain scene? I need a picture of a mountain so that I can use it for the front cover page of my new book."

"Awesome! Sure, I can!" he said. He then directed me to a place close by. About half-way to Stigler I approached a mountain, and as I topped it, I saw the perfect scene. I excitedly pulled my car over on the side of the road and started taking pictures with the digital camera

I had purchased earlier in the year. After I got home from church I transferred the pictures to my computer, but much to my dismay, they weren't close enough to see what I had wanted to capture. This camera didn't have a view screen or zoom lens, so I had missed the whole scene. At least, I found the physical mountain I was looking for.

Friday of that same week was Good Friday so our church was having a special Easter presentation. After work that day, I went to Wal-Mart to purchase the digital camera I needed. After praying about it, my eyes were drawn to a more expensive camera with a zoom lens and a viewing screen. I decided to purchase that one. I didn't have time to study about the camera and the digital concept was pretty new to me, so away to that mountain I drove again. I started taking pictures with the zoom but I soon ran out of space in the internal memory. I took a few more blind shots with my other camera, too. I eagerly anticipated the beautiful scenery as I downloaded the pictures onto my computer. But once again, I had missed that one special shot I had been looking for. I finally took some time to read and learn about my new camera and purchased a memory card for it for my next trip.

Easter Sunday after church, Heather and I headed back to the mountain. "Where are we going, Grandma?" she asked.

"We are going to go take a picture for the front cover of Grandma's book," I answered. She looked at me questioningly but enjoyed the ride. I spent quite a bit of time taking the pictures I thought would be the best, and I found that it was well worth the effort when I got home. I finally had the perfect shot of the mountains and valleys which accurately represented those of my life. It even had the cleared right of way which represented the path that the Lord had cleared for me to follow. I was very excited that now I could submit my manuscript, including the picture for the front cover.

"Thank You so much, Lord, for helping me to obtain the picture that will speak volumes to people, even as they just look at the cover! What an awesome God I serve!" I cried out joyfully.

After I submitted "Through the Valleys" to my publisher, a familiar restlessness stirred within my spirit as the Lord prepared me for the next season of my walk with Him. I had been watching Joyce Meyer on television almost every day since I totally surrendered my life to the Lord on December 31, 1997. Each year I prayed about going to her women's conference in St. Louis, Mo. I received a lot from her messages as she shared her life experiences and brought the truth of the scriptures to light. She was so down to earth and clearly gave the messages God had given her so that anyone could understand them. I could relate to her experiences in so many ways because I had a lot of the same issues in my life as she had dealt with in hers. I felt an urge in my heart to pray that God would make a way for me to go to her women's conference this year. Since I would soon be debt free and felt confident that God would answer my prayers, I started making plans to go. One evening God laid it on my heart to call my daughter Sandy to invite her to go with me to the conference. I had been praying for her to get closer to the Lord and for Him to do a work in her, but had no idea of how much He had already done until I called her.

"Hi, Babe, how would you like to go to St. Louis to a women's conference with me for a mother-daughter weekend?" I asked with some doubt.

"To the Joyce Meyer women's conference?" she asked.

I about fell out of my chair because I was shocked that she even knew about it. "Yes," I replied reluctantly.

"I would love to, Mom that sounds like so much fun!"

I was speechless for a moment or two as I tried to recover from the shock of her answer. "How did you know about it?" I asked.

"I and some of my friends have been talking about going. Do you care if one of my friends and her mother go with us?" she asked.

"No, I don't mind at all!" I responded.

"There is only one problem that I can foresee. Donny will be out on the road in the big truck and I don't drive in St. Louis!" she replied.

"I will come to pick you up and drive you to St. Louis then," I said. After I hung up the phone, I paid our registration and made the hotel reservations. I was so excited and I had no clue about the great things God was going to do at this conference.

The conference was held on Thursday, Friday, and Saturday. After work on Wednesday, I packed, loaded up the car, and headed for Illinois. After driving all night long, I arrived at Sandy's, took a short nap, we loaded her things in my car, and off we went. I was so excited and happy that she was going with me but I sensed that she was uneasy about this conference and even a little nervous about being with her "new mom". We checked into the hotel and went to McDonalds to eat before taking the bus to the conference center for the first session.

She hadn't ever been to a Pentecostal Charismatic church service before, so she was amazed as we started praise and worship in the freedom of the Holy Spirit that I was accustomed to. There were about 20,000 women all singing, clapping our hands, raising our hands to the Lord in worship and dancing. She looked around and saw everyone else doing the same, so she joined in by clapping. Shortly I saw the hand of God working on my precious beautiful daughter and she started enjoying everything just as much as I did.

While at the conference, tours of the St. Louis Dream Center were being scheduled and I felt an overwhelming desire to go. I signed up for a tour but Sandy said she was going to stay at the hotel and rest that day. After our group had loaded onto our bus to take the tour, Pam an intern from the Dream Center came on the bus. "Ladies and

Gentlemen, your tour has been cancelled because tornado warnings have been issued for this area," she sadly announced. "I am here to fill you in a little bit about the St. Louis Dream Center, which was established by Joyce and Dave Meyer." She shared several testimonies with us of lives that had been changed by this amazing outreach. As she told us of God's amazing love, grace, mercy, and blessings, I felt a very strong tug at my heart and I knew that the Lord was drawing me toward the Dream Center.

After everyone got off the bus and the intern was finally alone, I approached her for more information about the internship program she was involved in. I told her I was interested so she shared her testimony of how she had become involved with it. "Where do I go to get more information about it?"

"Just go back to the table where you signed up for the tour and ask for an application," she replied.

"No, I don't want an application just some information for now," I responded.

"The Lord says you want an application!" she replied.

Well, that was pretty straight forward and I knew that it had come from the Lord himself. I was quickly obedient to pick up an application to take home with me. When I got back to the hotel, I tried to explain it to Sandy. "The internship program is for singles who want to get involved in hands on ministry, those who are willing to trust God completely for the time it takes to get through the program, and are willing to give that part of their life totally to Him," I explained. She looked at me like I was crazy and for a while I felt like I was too. "I know this direction came from the Lord so I have to follow His lead and trust Him completely," I said to her confidently.

On the final day of the conference during worship, I saw the desperation in Sandy's eyes and the desire to have more of the relationship

I had with Jesus Christ. "Just stand up there and receive the precious gifts God wants to give you!" I told her. So up she got, hands uplifted to the heavens, and she received the fullness of the baptism of the precious Holy Spirit. Tears streamed down her face as God poured out His love upon her and I saw a new joy and peace come upon her.

I was overjoyed as the tears filled my eyes as well. "Thank You so much, Father God, for changing her life!" I knew she would never be the same again.

After I returned to Oklahoma, I completed the application and submitted all that was requested. It wasn't very long before I received a phone call from the staff at the Dream Center Ministry Academy for an interview. There were two program choices. So after prayer, I signed up for the summer Accelerate program in 2007. This program offered the same training as the nine month program but the time in each area of ministry was much less because the summer program was only nine weeks long.

Because the internship involvement included sixty to eighty hours per week, interns weren't allowed to work an outside job. This was a time to be totally dependent upon and devoted to God so He could prepare me for ministry.

The Lord had helped me to become almost debt free by this time, so I had no excuses regarding income. Since I had turned sixty-years old, and had been married to Don over ten years, I was eligible to draw Social Security widow's benefits from his account. I pursued this path and was quickly approved. One-hundred forty-nine dollars per month wasn't much but my tuition, meals, and housing were all included in the very reasonable price of the program. This small check would meet my personal needs while I was there. This desire was deeply ingrained in my spirit and heart and I knew it was God's direction for my life in this new season. As I prayed and sought the Lord's will in this whole new transition, He ministered to my heart. "You will have to give your home back to Bina and Doc. They will understand because I have already prepared their hearts," I heard Him say gently in my spirit.

"I had really hoped to return to my beautiful, comfortable, peaceful home near the lake and my job with Access Home Care, Lord, but nevertheless, Your will be done and not mine. You know the plans You have for me." I said with tears welling up in my eyes.

Whenever I started feeling down about letting go of the wonderfully blessed life I had in Checotah, the Holy Spirit always reminded me of the many times I gave up something to follow Jesus. I had always received even better blessings than I had before for being obedient. When I remembered those times, it wasn't nearly so hard to let go of the life I had become so comfortable with and enjoyed so much. It was still a challenge, though, and I won't say it was easy to give up my great hourly wage for the skimpy Social Security check I would be receiving, but I was very thankful that the Lord was providing something to meet my needs.

The director of the Ministry Academy had prepared me for the drastic changes of dormitory living with a dorm full of eighteen to twenty-four year-old young ladies, when I myself was sixty years young. As I pulled into the parking lot of the Dream Center that day in June, I was greeted warmly and lovingly by several of the interns. "Are you Barbara?" one of them asked inquisitively.

"Yes, I am," I answered rather overwhelmed by my welcoming group.

"I am Lorena, your roommate," She gave me a big hug. "I am very happy to meet you! You look a lot younger than I thought you would. I gave you the bottom bunk," she said as she helped me carry my clothes and things into our dorm room. Our room was very small with a large wardrobe, bunk beds, and a very small closet. She let me use the wardrobe while she used the small closet. This was quite a switch from the sixteen by seventy foot long mobile home that I had lived in and it was hard for me to fathom staying in this little room for very long. "I was afraid my roommate was going to be an old lady but I am pleasantly surprised. My mother has been praying for someone to share my room with me who will encourage and pray for me, and God has answered those prayers," Lorena said.

The next nine weeks were very physically and mentally challenging but they were a blessing and an eye opener. I got along great with all the girls and even gained three spiritual daughters. We were up taking a walk by 6:30 each morning; then on to praise and worship until 8 A.M., when we went to breakfast. We had classes in the mornings, served in outreaches in the afternoons, cleaned up the kitchen and cafeteria in the evenings, served in church services on Wednesday evenings, and somehow found time to study, too.

I was in awe of all the outreaches the Dream Center had for the neighborhoods and the homeless people. It was located in one of the highest crime areas of St. Louis where the greatest need was, so there was no lack of activity. There were two very large grills that a team took out several times a week to the parks, or just to the streets where they cooked hamburgers and hot dogs, and served drinks, chips, and cookies while they ministered the gospel to the people who came to enjoy the free food. One afternoon per week the interns were split up in teams to go visit people in their homes and tell them about our outreaches, pray with them, give them treats, and to share the love of God. On Friday evenings we separated into groups with the leaders of the Dream Center to go do street ministry. Some of the teams went to specific areas of the city while others just drove down the streets. We pulled over where we saw groups of people to share sandwiches, drinks, chips, cookies, and the gospel. My first time out on the street ministry, I went with an evangelist and we had sixty-two salvations in three hours. Wow!

After the street ministry teams returned, some of the interns joined in prayer, praise, and worship again to prepare spiritually for the midnight ministry. Teams took vans out to the liquor stores, motels, and bars to minister to the drug addicts, drug dealers, alcoholics, prostitutes, and anyone else that happened to be there.

We took roses to each of the prostitutes and when we approached them we told the ladies, "Jesus loves you and has a great plan for your life." It was amazing to watch the Lord touch their hearts and to see the hunger and desperation they had for a new lifestyle. On Saturdays we got up early to prepare for Kids Jam and the Adopt-A-Block outreaches. We had two Kids Jam trucks in which we carried sound equipment, games, food, tables, chairs, and whatever else we needed for these outreaches. Every Saturday each truck set up at two different locations where we fed the children and their parents while ministering the gospel through games, music, and other fun things. The Adopt-A-Block teams went from door to door in the neighborhood offering to help people do odd jobs, or whatever they needed done, which often included mowing the lawn for them. We shared the gospel with people we met on the streets and prayed with them. There were a lot of salvations through every outreach. On Sundays we got up early to serve at one church service in some way, and attended the second one for ourselves.

Sunday afternoons were spent cleaning our dorms and relaxing. The Dream Center was closed on Mondays so we always looked forward to some free time. Homeless people were bussed in from all over the city four days per week to get a hot meal, shower, change of clothing from our boutique, hair cut or shave, and for church services on Wednesday nights. There was also a nursing home ministry, from which a team went nearly every day to visit folks in different nursing homes to pray for them and fellowship with them. Tuesday evenings were special for all of us because our cafeteria was opened up, and the interns and staff served the homeless as if they were at a café. This ministry was called The D.C. Café. We each were assigned cleaning duties in the kitchen and dorms nightly, so we never got bored. It was very hard work but well worth the effort as we saw many hearts changed and souls saved. This opened my eyes to see the truth of what real ministry is and it's not just being in the pulpit, but much more about reaching out to others with the love of Jesus Christ and helping them any way they need to be helped.

After I had been at the ministry academy about two weeks, Mom had a bleeding ulcer and was admitted to the hospital. We almost lost her but the Lord performed a miracle by healing her body. My daughter, son-in-law, and granddaughters all made the trip to St. Louis on graduation day to watch me graduate and it was such a blessing to me.

As I prayed for God's direction after graduation, the Lord impressed upon my heart, "I want you to move back to Barry, Illinois so you can be close to your mother and your family." After about a month in the hospital, Mom moved in with my sister Rosemary in Quincy where she received physical therapy and home health services. I moved in with my daughter and her family until I could get a place of my own. I knew in my heart that this was God's plan to allow my granddaughters, daughter, and son-in-law get to know the "new me" because I had been out of the area for over thirteen years. It was a special time of bonding with my family and a time for me to get to know them as well.

Two months later I got my own apartment in the low- income government housing development right behind Sandy's home. I had applied for my Illinois nursing license right after graduation but the hindrances to getting it were huge and continuous, no matter how hard I prayed for the Lord to intervene. At the time I moved into my apartment, my income was only one-hundred forty- nine dollars per month, the widow's benefit from Social Security. The housing authority figured my rent at fifty dollars per month based on my income, which included utilities and trash pickup. I also received a small amount of food stamps from the state of Illinois to carry me through. I never dreamed I could live on such a small income but, after tithing on my small check, the Lord stretched what I had so much that I was never completely broke. As I gave my tithes and offering at church each month, the scripture about the "widows mite" (Luke 21:1-4) kept coming to me. My mind still cannot comprehend how all that works out, but that's where faith comes into play, by trusting God to meet all my needs (Philippians 4:19).

I kept searching for jobs I thought I could do while waiting for the State of Illinois to reinstate my nursing license. Finally, right before Thanksgiving, I got a temporary position at the Wal-Mart Supercenter in Hannibal, Missouri in the toy department. Since my granddaughters were all teens now, it had been years since I even thought about toys. I knew almost nothing about the new ones. This job required a lot of prayer and grace because it was not only emotionally taxing but physically as well. I had never worked in the retail business before so it was truly out of my comfort zone but since God had opened this door, I gave it my best. I found it very challenging to walk in love and in the Spirit, especially during the Christmas season when emotions ran high and the stress level was unbelievable. The lack of respect for others in this new generation was really hard for me to deal with, but thanks to the grace of God, I made it through this season of my life and managed to share the love of Christ with others. I found that I had a new respect and vision of the people who work there all the time. I appreciate them much more now and I often let them know it.

Finally, toward the middle of December 2007, my Illinois nursing license arrived so I started searching for a nursing position. One day when I went to Rosemary's to visit Mom her case manager from the home health agency came to see her while I was there. The Lord prompted me to ask her if the agency needed any nurses. "I just turned in my resignation so I know they do. Why don't you go put in an application?" Quickly the door opened for an L.P.N. position at the adult day care services located in the Senior Citizens building in Quincy, Illinois. The pay wasn't as much as I would have liked but it was Monday through Thursday for ten hours per day with three-day weekends off. That part I really enjoyed and was very thankful for.

Commuting to work sixty miles per day was piling up the mileage on my car, which now had well over two-hundred thousand miles on it but it was paid for. Little things started going wrong with it. I prayed for the Lord to help it last longer. One day He spoke to my spirit and said, "You had better use wisdom. Cars weren't built to last forever."

I had hoped to be able to retire from nursing at age sixty-two so I could start writing the books God had placed in my heart, so I tried reasoning with Him.

"God, You know if I have a car payment to make, I can't afford to retire." I knew that He had other plans. I was sure that He knew what was best for me. I finally surrendered and started looking for a new car. He had been ministering to me about more traveling opportunities, which I had been praying for, so I understood that I needed a newer, more dependable vehicle. As I prayed for direction and guidance, He led me to Royal Oaks Nissan in Springfield, where I met some great Christian men to help me, including the salesman and the financial director. I wanted a brand new car but since a new one was out of my price range, I settled for a 2006 Nissan Sentra with low mileage, full factory warranty, extended warranty, and a lifetime bumper to bumper power train warranty. Amazingly, it was very much like the 2001 Nissan Sentra I traded in, except this one was upgraded. It still had all my little compartments and conveniences I had and enjoyed in my old car. At least now, I had the reassurance that if anything went wrong with this one, there were warranties to cover the repairs. Once more, God had blessed me abundantly with just what I had asked Him for in this great little car and He had worked out the financing on it to suit my budget, too. Before I drove it off the dealer's lot, I prayed over it, anointed it, dedicated it to God's service, just as I did everything now and thanked Him for His many blessings.

I had felt led to do daily devotionals with some of the clients at the Adult Day Care Center, and they really enjoyed it and looked forward to it. One day, my boss came to me and asked to have a word with me. "You can't minister to the people here anymore. It is inappropriate and you are a nurse," she said. Apparently someone had taken offense. I felt as if someone had pierced my heart with a sword and discontentment with my position hit me like a ton of bricks.

I started praying for the Lord to give me a position closer to home to save mileage, time, and wear and tear on me and my new car. In May of 2008, He opened the door for a position as an L.P.N. at the nursing home in Barry. I started out making three dollars more on the hour than at the day care, with benefits. At first, I wasn't too happy about working the evening shift but soon I found that it was more convenient for me to have the mornings to write or do whatever God wanted me to do. Not only that, I lived only five minutes from work, which made it much better because I had more time at home.

It wasn't what I really wanted to do but the Lord has used me many times to share His love with others by just being the person that I have become through my personal relationship with Him. I didn't know how much difference I was making in people's lives until I heard the comments that some of the family members and other staff members had made to other people about me and my life with Jesus. It is so beautiful and a great blessing to know that I have made a difference in someone's day or life, and that God has chosen this humble vessel to use for that purpose. I am very careful to give Him all the glory because without Him I could do nothing, but I can do all things through Christ who strengthens me (Philippians 4:12-13).

I am now looking forward to the next season of my life. God opened the doors for me to attend a Christian Writers Conference in Florida in February 2009 where I had my manuscript critiqued by an editor. I believe with my whole heart that God is taking me in a completely new direction with the divine connections and appointments He had for me there. I am so thankful that I am truly prosperous in the kingdom of God with all the fruit of the spirit working within me, which are love, joy, peace, patience, kindness, goodness, faithfulness, gentleness, and self-control (Galatians 5:22-23). True "Kingdom Prosperity" is flowing in the gifts of the spirit which are: messages of wisdom and knowledge, faith, gifts of healing, miraculous powers, prophecy, discernment of spirits, speaking in other tongues, and interpretation of tongues (1 Corinthians 12:8-10).

My natural gifts of a warm, beautiful home with modern conveniences and comforts, a great economical dependable car, my family, loved ones, friends, wonderful loving church family, my health, and many other blessings too numerous to mention also contribute to the "Kingdom Prosperity" in which I now live.

So now you see, my friend, that "Kingdom Prosperity" is much more than just money and material possessions. It all starts with a personal relationship with Jesus Christ by surrendering your life to Him and being obedient to His word and His spirit. When you seek the kingdom of God first and all His righteousness, all these things shall be added unto you (Luke 12:31).

abundantly! Now that I have shared my experiences and my heart with you, you can see that prosperity is much more than just material possessions and money. It is an abundance of peace, love, joy, health, sound mind, forgiveness, wholeness, and the confidence of knowing who you are and why you are here on this earth.

You, too, can have this freedom and enjoy the Lord's prosperity by surrendering your life to Him and living the abundant life He has purposed for you to live. When you live by His principles and do your very best to serve Him with what He has given you, He will help you be set free from the chains of bondage to debt and sin. He loves you so much and He is no respecter of persons, so what He has done for me; He will also do for you if you make that choice and ask Him.

If you have been enlightened by this book and are ready to make the choice to surrender to Jesus, pray this simple prayer and mean it sincerely from your heart:

"Dear Jesus, I am a sinner in need of a Savior. I repent of my sins and ask You to forgive me. I believe that You are the Son of God, You lived and died for my salvation, and You were raised from the dead on the third day. Thank You, Lord, for paying my sin debt for me. Come into my life and be my Lord. Help me to follow You in Jesus' name. Amen."

Congratulations! You are now a child of the Most High God. Welcome to the family of God!

Now, find a good Bible based church to attend regularly, pray, worship Him, and study your Bible daily. You will be amazed at how quickly your whole life will change for the better and how quickly you too begin to walk in true prosperity!

I welcome your prayer requests, comments, and suggestions. You may write to me at: 101 N 4th St, Apt. 604, Quincy, IL 62301, or by e-mail at: barbaragore368@yahoo.com. You can also contact me through

my Wings of Love Ministry Facebook page at: www.facebook.com/
wingsofloveministry.

My currently published books: *Whispers from Heaven,* a collection
of prophecies and poetry, and *Through the Valleys,* my autobiography,
are available through me personally, at buybooksontheweb.com, and
most major bookstores by special order. *Reflections of God's Love,* my
next book of Christian poetry and prophecies, is coming soon so watch
for my announcement!

Thank you for allowing me the honor and privilege of sharing my
life and insights with you. I hope this book has helped you to see what
true "Kingdom Prosperity" is and has sharpened your desire for it, too.
When you have Jesus as your Lord and Savior, you are truly rich! May
God bless you

www.ingramcontent.com/pod-product-compliance
Lightning Source LLC
Chambersburg PA
CBHW021002150626
46549CB00012BA/776